THE POWER OF A

Praying®

Nation

Global Edition

STORMIE OMARTIAN

HARVEST HOUSE PUBLISHERS
Eugene, Oregon 97402

Cover by Koechel Peterson & Associates, Minneapolis, Minnesota

THE POWER OF A PRAYING® NATION GLOBAL EDITION
Copyright © 2002 by Stormie Omartian
Published by Harvest House Publishers
Eugene, Oregon 97402

Library of Congress Cataloging-in-Publication Data
ISBN 0-7369-1030-1

Printed in the United States of America.

02   03   04   05   06   07   08   09   10   /   BP-MS   /   10   9   8   7   6   5   4   3   2   1

This book is dedicated to the many men and women who gave their lives in defense of America's freedom, or who were in the line of fire when the enemy attacked, or were killed trying to save the lives of others. In gratitude for their supreme sacrifice, I pray God's peace, comfort, and blessing upon the family members and loved ones they left behind. May God fill that empty place in their lives with His healing and restoring love.

Acknowledgments

With special thanks:

✍♥ To Pastor Jack Hayford and Pastor Rice Broocks for teaching me how to not only pray for *our* nation, but for *all* the nations of the world.

✍♥ To my husband, Michael, for encouraging me to write this book.

✍♥ To Susan Martinez for being the best secretary, assistant, prayer partner, sister, and friend, and feeling the stress of deadlines as much as I do.

✍♥ To Roz Thompson for being a loyal friend, prayer partner, encourager, and supporter, especially during the writing of this project.

✍♥ To my Harvest House family, especially Bob Hawkins Jr., Carolyn McCready, Terry Glaspey, Julie McKinney, Teresa Evenson, Betty Fletcher, LaRae Weikert, John Constance, and Peggy Wright for your hard work and unwavering support.

✍♥ To Stephen McDowell and Mark Beliles from the Providence Foundation for all your work in preserving the true greatness of our nation's history in your book *America's Providential History*. If everyone were to read this work, there could be no doubt that our country was founded, established, built, and made strong by men and women of prayer who followed after God. May it inspire us as a nation to continue in that tradition.

Contents

Preface
The Power of a Praying Nation
Global Edition

Because God has answered my prayers, my books are now translated into many different languages and are available all over the world. So you may be reading this in a language other than English, which is my native language, and in a country other than the United States, which is the country where I was born. If so, I find this very exciting. That's because I know when you pray for *your* country as I do for mine, you too can expect to see the hand of God powerfully move in response to your prayers.

There is not a nation on earth that couldn't profoundly benefit from the prayers of believers united in faith. What country hasn't endured some kind of tragedy or difficulty requiring the kind of help that can only come from God in response to fervent intercession? And who knows the number of serious situations that could have been *prevented* if people had been praying strategically in advance. You and I, and anyone else who will join us, have the opportunity to affect the course of any nation for which we pray. And we need to take advantage of that opportunity, because what happens in any part of the world today will ultimately affect us all, no matter where we are.

Jesus aid, "Blessed are the peacemakers, for they shall be called sons of God" (Matthew 5:9). Prayer warriors and intercessors *are* peacemakers. That's because prayer aligns us with God, who is the ultimate Peacemaker, and when we pray we become a channel through which He can bring peace to wherever we direct our prayers. By joining in prayer as the body of believers worldwide, we can be a part of God's healing, guiding, delivering, and restoring process. Who knows what a positive difference we can make in our world!

—Stormie Omartian

Give heed to the voice of my cry,
my King and my God, for to You I will pray...
For You are not a God who takes pleasure
in wickedness, nor shall evil dwell with You...
But let all those rejoice who put their trust in You;
Let them ever shout for joy, because You defend them.

PSALM 5:2,4,11

CHAPTER
ONE

When Tragedy
Hits Home

I woke up at 3:30 in the morning on September 11, 2001, with a deep feeling of dread, overwhelming sadness, and suffocating oppression. It was so heavy on me that it felt like the weight of the world. At first I thought something terrible must have happened or that someone had died. I'd awakened with a similar feeling several years before on the morning after the sudden tragic death of a close friend. Yet I don't even recall that feeling being as strong as what I was experiencing at this particular moment. But to my knowledge no one had died, and nothing terrible had happened.

I realized I needed to pray, but I didn't know exactly what to pray about. So I started with praying for each of my children and my husband. I knew they were safe in their beds at that time, but I thought perhaps there was something looming out ahead that I should pray about in advance. I didn't have any clear leading about that, so I moved on to other loved ones. I prayed for my dad, sister, brothers-and-sisters-in-law, nieces, nephews, aunts, and uncles. I prayed for friends one by one and each of their family members. I prayed for myself. *Was the trip I was going to be taking out of the country something to be concerned about?* Still no relief. Still no answer. Still no peace.

"Has something terrible happened that I don't know about?" I asked God. "Is something bad *about* to happen? What is this heavy oppression, Lord?"

There was still no answer, so I kept on praying as the Spirit led. It was quite some time before I was finally able to fall asleep again. As a result, I slept much later than usual. I didn't even hear my husband, Michael, get up and make coffee in the kitchen. Shortly after 9:00 A.M. he burst into the bedroom and woke me from a deep sleep.

"Stormie, you have to get up and see this," he said as he grabbed the remote from the small table on the other side of the bedroom and turned on the TV.

"An airplane hit one of the World Trade Center towers, and as I was watching the news coverage, another plane ran right into the other tower," he urgently explained. "They are both on fire."

"Oh God, help us," I said as I got up and moved to where I could see the television more clearly. What he described was being replayed at that very moment. The sight was sickening and shocking, almost too horrible to believe.

"God help the people in these buildings," Michael and I prayed together in desperation. "Save everyone who is still alive. Rescue those in the upper floors who have no way out. Help them to evacuate the lower floors."

We sat glued to the television, paralyzed by the horror of what we saw.

My mind flashed back to the last time I stood in front of these same buildings. I remembered looking up at their mammoth stature and being struck with how solid and breathtakingly beautiful they were.

Those towers are girded about with steel, I thought as I continued to watch the television. *They withstood that last enormous bombing at the site of their very foundation. Surely they will* hold now. *If the fires can be confined to the upper floors then certainly the floors below will be spared.*

We continued to pray as the tragedy kept unfolding. The news reported another jetliner had crashed into the Pentagon. There were more deaths and more destruction. It was clear by that time that America was under attack and the plan was to destroy as many people and high-profile landmarks as possible using fuel-heavy aircraft as bombs.

"Dear God, put a stop to this evil destruction," we prayed in desperation. "End this attack on our country. If there are more planes headed for other targets, stop them immediately. Halt this onslaught of terror. Protect President Bush. Hide him in Your shadow, Lord, where no weapon formed against his life will prosper. Give him wisdom to make quick decisions."

As horrifying as all these events were, nothing in our worst nightmare or wildest thoughts prepared us for what we witnessed next; when suddenly one of the enormous 110-story World Trade Center towers collapsed completely to the ground in a heap of burning rubble. Thousands of people who had not already died in the fire and smoke of the upper floors were now carried to their deaths. The unimaginable horror was impossible to believe. We sat frozen in shock, stricken by the overwhelming magnitude of this unfathomable catastrophe.

"This can't be happening," I cried as we sat in stunned silence, watching it over and over. "Oh Lord, save anyone who might still be alive."

We were then notified by a news report that another aircraft had crashed outside of Pittsburgh, Pennsylvania. And in Washington, D.C., part of the Pentagon had collapsed. More unsuspecting people met a violent death.

Twenty minutes later the other World Trade Center tower collapsed like its twin in a burning, billowing, blinding heap of rubble. Thousands more lives were lost. We and the nation watched the events again and again, as if by doing so we could make ourselves comprehend them. But it was a tragedy beyond comprehension. Through our tears and shock we tried to get our arms around the enormity of it all, but it was just too big. We hoped to wake up from this nightmare. But we never did. We had awakened *to* a nightmare instead. And this nightmare was just beginning.

We looked for signs of hope and kept praying that by some miracle people were still alive in the rubble or in the mall under ground. "Lord, keep those people alive until rescue workers can get to them," I prayed over and over.

Another news report informed us that the four crashed planes had been hijacked commercial jetliners. Each one had *passengers* on them. It was another devastating realization that more unsuspecting, innocent people had been killed in a most brutal and terrifying way.

Then came the news that hundreds of firefighters and police officers were lost in the collapse of the World Trade Center towers. *Hundreds!* Hundreds of brave, heroic men and women lost their lives trying to save the lives of others. Was there no end to bad news on this day? The grief was unbearable. It felt like the weight of the world.

The weight of the world!

At that moment, I remembered awakening in the middle of the night with the same terrible, oppressive feeling. And suddenly I realized what that was all about.

"Oh Lord, You were calling me to pray for our country, but I didn't get it," I said. I prayed for myself and my loved ones, but I didn't think to pray for my country. I had learned years ago the importance of praying for the nation's leaders, especially the president of the United States. I had been praying fervently for President George W. Bush from the time he was elected because I had this strong, unshakeable, undeniable feeling that he would be the target of a would-be assassin. My prayer group, the women who meet weekly in my home, felt that way too, and so we faithfully prayed for his protection each time we were together. But never did we think to pray about a terrorist attack on our land. That possibility just seemed too remote.

In the days that followed, the nation woke up each morning with heavy hearts. But as the initial paralysis of grief wore off, we became determined to do something about the forces of evil that had caused this destruction so that they could never do such a thing to anyone again. We rallied behind our president, confident that he was the right man at the right time. His compassion and unflinching determination to bring the perpetrators to justice gave us strength. And he had by his side many gifted, knowledgeable, godly, and wise men and women who were capable of getting the job done.

America declared war on those responsible for this horrible act. But it would be a war like no other. There were no boundary lines for the enemy who hid and preyed on the helpless and innocent. The thousands of lives that were destroyed on September 11 were not soldiers on a battlefield. They were civilians who said goodbye to their loved ones that morning, never dreaming it would be for the last time. They were fathers and mothers, husbands and wives, sons and daughters, brothers and sisters, aunts and uncles, cousins, grandparents, and friends who would never come home again.

Now there were numbers of children left without a father or mother to love them. There were mothers and fathers without the son or daughter they had sacrificed their lives to raise. Brothers, sisters, family members, loved ones, friends, valued acquaintances, coworkers, employers, employees, business partners and associates were now forever bereft of the people who gave their lives meaning. As we heard each new heartbreaking story of tragic loss we cried all over again. We mourned with those who mourned. We tried to have hope along with those who still hoped their loved ones would be found. People everywhere extended themselves to do whatever they could to help. But whatever we did never seemed like enough. The loss was too great. The destruction too massive.

Of all the many horrific aspects of that tragic day, it seems like the moment the first World Trade Center building fell something fell in our hearts as well. It was the end of an era. The things in life we thought could never fall did. And something fell in us too.

We realized how desperately we needed God. Prayer suddenly became the right thing to do. God got invited back into our public gathering places. People saw that they couldn't handle life without Him after all. There were many gut-wrenching questions about why this had happened, and people looked to God for the answers. They found prayer was an answer that had been forgotten for too long.

For weeks afterwards, I couldn't stop crying over the senseless loss of life, and for the families and loved ones who grieved for them. Indeed all Americans cried together. If God really does keep our tears in a bottle, as the psalmist suggests (Psalm 56:8), then heaven must have been flooded in the aftermath of that morning. Our flow of combined tears became a mighty river of unity like we had not known before in this country. It flowed out to others, even to strangers on the streets. And it flowed back to us in the outpouring of love and compassion from people all over the world who shared our grief.

We who witnessed these events will never be the same. We witnessed the unimaginable. We were exposed to incomprehensible evil. We watched thousands of people disintegrate in front of our eyes. We may have gone back about our business because we had to, but it will never be business as usual again. We look at each other differently now. With new eyes of appreciation. With new eyes of suspicion. We may have resumed our lives, but our minds contain the knowledge that something bad could happen at any time. We've gone back to building for tomorrow, but we can't be certain what tomorrow will bring.

Anyone who doubted the existence of evil can't deny it any longer. They've seen it in action. Even the pictures of ground zero, with the endless smoke rising over mass destruction, resembled what hell must surely look like. Satan had left his imprint. His destructive design for our lives was revealed in the rubble, in the ashes of lives that are no more.

Have we cried our last tear over this horrible event in our nation's history? I hope not. Will we get to the point where we can see our flag or hear our national anthem and forget all it meant and symbolized for us in the days following September 11? I hope not. Will we take for granted the freedom for which thousands of brave men and women have given their lives over the years? Will we again feel so secure that we think we don't have to look to God as a nation anymore? I pray not.

Even as our lives return to normal, we must never forget what happened. To remember will remind us to pray like we have never prayed before. If the memories of that day can inspire us to become prayer warriors strong enough to turn our nation toward God, then the thousands of victims of that dark morning will not have died in vain.

We who know God have heard His call to pray, and it has awakened in us a whole new sense of urgency. But it must also broaden our scope. When I heard His call to pray early that morning, I was only thinking in terms of my own little world. God wants us to think in terms of praying for our nation and the nations of the world. Our prayers must not only cover our own land, but they must also reach around the globe.

Regarding *how* to pray, God knows that "we do not know what we should pray for as we ought, but the Spirit Himself makes intercession for us with groanings which cannot be uttered" (Romans 8:26). In other words, we won't always know the specifics of what we need to pray for, but the Holy Spirit will help us. I remember in that middle-of-the-night prayer session when I didn't know what more to pray about, I felt led to pray the Lord's Prayer. Who knows if the words "Your will be done on earth" and "deliver us from evil" might have saved even one person's life that day? The Holy Spirit knows and will lead us when we ask Him to.

As to why I didn't hear from God about specifics of how to pray on that early morning when I was awakened out of a sound sleep, I believe the answer lies in the fact that I had not been praying along those lines in recent months. Even though I had been taught how to intercede for my country, I had fallen out of the habit. And there was good reason for that. I had been dealing with a life-threatening illness and though I had nearly recovered physically, I was still trying to recover my life, which had gone speeding on by me during my long convalescence. I had not been asking God to show me how to pray for my country and its leaders. My mind and heart were not there, and so I was not sensitive to that.

But in addition to the specific prayers in a moment of great need, there are also prayers we can pray on a regular basis that will cover our nation and help us to become the intercessors God is calling us to be. And if any group of people join together in these prayers, they can become a powerful praying nation. This book is about those prayers.

Today there is a hole in the heart of our nation that only God can fill. We have a pain in our souls that only God can heal. Our country is weighed down with a burden of grief that only God can carry. He wants to do all that and more. And He wants to do this not only for *my* nation, but for *every* nation in the world. There are deep wounds in the heart of *many* nations that need to be healed. God wants to bring new life where there has been death. He wants to bring restoration where there has been loss. He wants to not only raise us up again, but to take us to new heights. But that can only happen if we turn to Him with a humble and pure heart, seek His face and His ways, and pray like never before.

Let's do all that so we can unite our countries in prayer and see the power of God move on our behalf. Let's ask for the peace of God to bless our own countries and the nations of the world with peace. And let us continue in prayer to fight for liberty and justice for all.

Prayer Power

Lord, I pray for the people of my country to find healing for the memories of the terrible tragedies that have happened in our land. I pray especially for those who have lost loved ones. Give them a greater sense of Your presence so that they may find Your comfort. Provide for their every need. As we weep with those who weep, help us to bear their burdens in prayer. Pour Your healing love over them so they will know Your peace. As we recover from any tragic time, help us to not forget to "pray without ceasing" for our nation to be protected (1 Thessalonians 5:17). Help us to remember that the only things in this world that are indestructible are You and Your Word.

Your Word tells us that there will be cataclysmic events that will happen in the world, but I pray that there will be an end to disasters or tragedies in our nation. Even if those kinds of events do occur again, I pray that You would protect us in the midst of them. Turn the heart of our nation toward You. Awaken in us a new realization of our need for Your guidance and protection. Give us a new understanding of what is really important. Comfort us in our affliction with the life of Your Word (Psalm 119:50). Your Word says that You have "borne our griefs and carried our sorrows" (Isaiah 53:4). Bear our grief now and make it count for something. Carry our sorrow and turn it into good for future generations. Put gladness in our hearts once again.

Lord, teach me how to be a powerful intercessor for my nation and the nations of the world. Help me to pray consistently and with great understanding. Give me revelation and insight that guides my prayers so that I may pray more effectively. Help the believers of this nation to rise up together and learn to pray in power. Enable us to teach our children how to pray for their nation as well, and help us all to understand what it means to be a nation whose God is the Lord. In Jesus' name I pray.

WEAPONS OF WARFARE

Blessed are those who mourn,
for they shall be comforted.
MATTHEW 5:4

The people who walked in darkness have seen a great light; those who dwelt in the land of the shadow of death, upon them a light has shined.
ISAIAH 9:2

The sun shall no longer be your light by day, nor for brightness shall the moon give light to you; but the LORD will be to you an everlasting light, and your God your glory ....and the days of your mourning shall be ended.
ISAIAH 60:19-20

This is my comfort in my affliction,
for Your word has given me life.
PSALM 119:50

The effective, fervent prayer
of a righteous man avails much.
JAMES 5:16

CHAPTER TWO

Why Bad Things Happen to Innocent People

We all question why bad things happen to decent, honest, good people while murderers go free. We all wonder why the drunk driver comes out of the car he was driving without a scratch on him while the woman and child he hit lie dead in the street. We have a strong sense of justice, and we don't like it when life is not fair to us or to others. "Why?" "Why?" We say it over and over. In the aftermath of the September 11 tragedy in America, everyone was asking why. I'm sure there have been tragedies in *every* nation at one time or another that have caused people to ask why.

One of the most frequently asked questions following these horrible events in our nation was "Why did God allow this to happen?" There were many variations on that question, some of which may seem outlandish to those of us who understand the true nature of God, but they were asked by people who were devastated and overwhelmed with grief and fear. They needed answers to help them survive. Here are some of the questions I heard people ask, along with some brief answers I think we need to consider.

1. Why Did God Do This?

God didn't do this, *people* did.

2. Why Did This Happen?

It happened because there is evil in the world. People who open themselves up to the influence of evil end up being ruled by it. The perpetrators of these crimes were operating under the influence of evil. There is no end to what evil can do if it is organized and left unchallenged.

3. Why Is There So Much Evil in the World?

I've heard some people say that they don't believe God exists because they see so much evil in the world. But I tell them that if God didn't exist, they would see *nothing else but evil* in the world. The fact they see any love, joy, compassion, generosity, order, peace, rest, health, clarity of mind, or fulfillment is because God exists. The reason there is evil in the world is because so many people are willing to reject the one true God and rebel against His ways. They follow instead after their fleshly desires and the ways of the devil.

4. Why Doesn't God Get Rid of Evil?

God hates evil. He hates sin. If He got rid of all evil in the world, He'd have to get rid of all of us because we all have some evil or sin in our hearts. But God has a plan to get rid of evil one person at a time. He sent Jesus to earth to fulfill that plan. Jesus paid the price of our sin, which is death. He died in our place so that we can be redeemed and restored. When we receive Jesus, God deposits the Holy Spirit in our hearts. The Holy Spirit cleanses our hearts from the inside out and gives us the power to resist evil.

Although God is sovereign, He does not force His will upon us. He leaves our decisions up to us. He wants us to make the right decisions, to use the authority He has given us to bring evil under control. He asks us not to support evil, not join forces with it, and not cheer it on. He wants us to become aware of the tactics evil uses, resist evil when we see it, separate ourselves from it, and make laws to control or eliminate it whenever it manifests itself. Prayer is the primary means God gives us to accomplish all that.

5. Why Did God Allow This?

God has set up certain laws on earth, and He will not violate them. For example, He does not go against the laws of nature, such as the law of gravity or cause and effect. There are also laws of human nature, and one of these concerns our free will. Even though God is all-powerful, He has chosen to give control over what happens on earth to *us*. And one of the most powerful means by which we control things on earth is through prayer. We pray and ask God to intervene. He acts in response to our asking. The prayers of those who believe in and love Him are His primary tools for impacting our world. If we don't ask, there can be no answer. We allow evil to proliferate when we don't resist it or pray about it. We move out from under God's protective covering when we don't live His way and seek His protection.

Jesus said, "I will give you the keys of the kingdom of heaven, and whatever you bind on earth will be bound in heaven, and whatever you loose on earth will be loosed in heaven" (Matthew 16:19). *Binding* and *loosing* have to do with *forbidding* and *permitting*. Through this kind of praying, God has given us the means by which we can forbid evil to control our lives, and permit God to be in charge. So why don't we pray this way? One reason may be our unwillingness to acknowledge that evil exists. Another might be our unwillingness to acknowledge that God exists. Or it could be that we are afraid of having Him interfere with our lives. Or maybe we don't really believe that God actually cares about us or that prayer really works.

6. Why Wasn't God Around When This Tragedy Occurred?

God is always where He is invited to be. If He is not asked to come into a situation or into the lives of people, He will not be there in power. Yes, it's true that God is everywhere, but He does not manifest His power to the fullest if He is not asked to do so. For example, when Jesus taught us how to pray, He gave us the Lord's Prayer as a model. In that prayer our all-knowing God, who knows everything we need, tells us to ask for our daily bread. If He knows that we need food, why does He still want us to ask for it? In that same prayer our all-powerful God, who has the power to destroy evil in the twinkling of an eye, still asks us to pray that we be delivered from evil. Why does He do that? Because one of His principles is that we should ask and He will answer.

God asks us to *pray* to Him for the things we need in our lives. He wants us to partner with Him to guide what happens on earth. If we need God to intervene in a situation, and it appears that He is nowhere to be found, it's probably because no one asked Him to be there in power. Whenever people want God to leave them alone, He will. If it seems God is absent from a situation, it's our fault, not His. It's because we have not invited Him to be there in power. When we all finally started praying on September 11 we partnered with God to bring His full power to bear on the situation, helping thousands of people to safety who might otherwise have perished.

7. Why Do Bad Things Happen to Innocent People?

Bad things like what happened on September 11 don't happen because the victims who died were evil or bad. If that were the case, why are the rest of us still alive? When people asked Jesus whether the bad things that happened to certain people were because of their individual sins, He said no. He then gave the example of the tower in Siloam that fell and killed eighteen people. "Those eighteen on whom the tower in Siloam fell and killed them, do you think that they were worse sinners than all other men who dwelt in Jerusalem? I tell you, no; but unless you repent you will all likewise perish" (Luke 13:4-5).

The key word here is *repent*. The point is, we all deserve to die for our sins. *Sin* is an old archery term that means anything that is not right on target in the center of the bull's-eye. Without God, we are all off center. We miss the mark to which God calls us. But Jesus gave His life so that by putting our faith in Him and *repenting* of our sin, we could receive full forgiveness. He paid the price for our sins, but we have to receive Him in order to take advantage of it. Even after we receive the Lord, we still sometimes miss the mark. We still do things for which we need to repent.

Are the sins of those who perished in the World Trade Center towers or the Pentagon or any of the hijacked planes any greater than yours or mine? God says no. There is nothing those people did to deserve that horrible and terrifying death any more than what you or I have done.

Only God knows why some people die at certain times and not others. We know that many died in the World Trade Center towers assisting others to safety. Some people may have been helping severely injured men and women find God in their final moments. These people sacrificed their own lives for the lives of others and have now found an eternal reward. And we don't know how many people cried out to God in Jesus' name to save them just before they died. But we know God heard their prayers and opened the gates of heaven for them.

8. Why Didn't God Warn Us?

God did warn us. We may not have been given specifics about that particular tragedy, but He has been warning us for years. For one thing, His warnings are all over the Bible. He said through the apostle Paul that we must "stand against the wiles" of the enemy who "walks about like a roaring lion seeking whom he may devour" (Ephesians 6:11; 1 Peter 5:8). But how many of us stand against him when things are going well? The apostle James exhorts us to "Submit to God. Resist the devil and he will flee from you" (James 4:7). But how many of us actually submit and resist on a consistent basis? God says,

"If My people who are called by My name will humble themselves, and pray and seek my face, and turn from their wicked
ways, then I will hear from heaven, and will forgive their sin
and heal their land" (2 Chronicles 7:14). How many of us
have humbled ourselves in repentance for our sins and the sins
of our nation? How many of us are brokenhearted about the
things we tolerate in our nation that break the heart of God?
How often do we seek His face and pray that we as a people
will turn from our wicked ways?

God has warned us that we have an enemy who wants to
destroy us. Most people try hard to make the world a better
place, but Satan and those who do his bidding continually
labor to destroy such good work. There are good men and
women who spend their lives trying to rid the world of diseases.
But evil men work hard to build arsenals of germs and chemi-
cals to infect and kill millions of people. There are men and
women who design and build places of beauty, strength, and
protection where we can live and work in safety. But evil men
spend their days thinking up ways to tear them down. God has
warned us that the devil is always making plans for death and
destruction, and we need to resist his efforts by our actions and
our prayers. But many of us don't heed the warnings.

God often uses other people to warn us. For years we have
heard experts say that the next great threat to our country
would be terrorism. Did we pray as we ought to have about it? Is
it possible that God *did* warn us about September 11 but we were
too wrapped up in our own lives to hear it? And how many spiritual leaders in our country, strong men and women of God,
have warned us that we need to repent and pray on behalf of our
nation? The warnings were there. A number of godly men and
women heard them. But most of us either didn't hear or we
ignored what we heard.

9. Why Shouldn't I Blame God for What Happened?

Many people shut God out of their lives by blaming Him
for the bad things that happen. But this is the biggest mistake

anyone could make. That's because disaster comes to people who blame God for the pain in their lives. "Happy is the man who is always reverent, but he who hardens his heart will fall into calamity" (Proverbs 28:14). And when our hearts grow hard toward God, we shut off the very avenue by which blessings can come to us. Then we wonder why God is not answering our prayers.

No matter what is happening around us or to us, we must trust God's love for us in the midst of it. Lack of trust on our part makes us wonder whether God actually has our best interests at heart. Then we become mad at Him when bad things happen. Rather than blaming God, let's cast blame on the one who deserves it. He is the enemy who endlessly schemes and plots to fulfill his evil plans against us.

These are just a few of the many questions that people need to have answered. Let's pray that we will have the right answers when we are asked, and that our answers will be given in love and compassion, with words that communicate God's heart. Let's pray for ears and hearts to be open to hear the truth. Let's pray for God's protection for innocent people. And let's invite the God of all comfort to comfort those who have been hurt by tragedy and draw them close to Himself.

Prayer Power

Lord, my heart grieves over the many terrible things that have happened to innocent people in my country and throughout the world. It must grieve Your heart even more because You know the promise that each life held and the purpose for which You created them. Thank You, Lord, that You are not a distant God. You are with us and care about our suffering. "You, O Lord, are a God full of compassion, and gracious, longsuffering and abundant in mercy and truth" (Psalm 86:15). You are a good and loving God, and all Your paths for those who love You and seek Your wisdom and understanding are "paths of peace" (Proverbs 3:13-17). Take the blinders off of us as a nation, and help us to be a people who are undeceived about who You are. Help us to see that You are on our side and are not the author of evil deeds. Help us to recognize who our enemy really is.

God, we cannot bear to see anything happen again on this earth like the tragedies that we have witnessed in different parts of our world. I pray that you would put an end to mass destruction and catastrophic loss of life in our country and everywhere else on earth. Wake up Your people to pray and help us to hear Your call. Teach us as a nation to intercede on behalf of all people everywhere. Enable us to be intercessors after Your own heart. Help me, along with my brothers and sisters in Christ, to have the right answers at the right time for those who have hard questions. May our answers be given in such a loving way that people are comforted and You are lifted up and glorified. In Jesus' name I pray.

WEAPONS OF WARFARE

These things I have spoken to you, that in Me you may have peace. In the world you will have tribulation; but be of good cheer, I have overcome the world.
JOHN 16:33

God will wipe away every tear from their eyes; there shall be no more death, nor sorrow, nor crying. There shall be no more pain, for the former things have passed away.
REVELATION 21:4

Let us therefore come boldly to the throne of grace, that we may obtain mercy and find grace to help in time of need.
HEBREWS 4:16

This is the confidence that we have in Him,
that if we ask anything according to His will, He hears us.
1 JOHN 5:14

Evil men and impostors will grow worse and worse, deceiving and being deceived. But you must continue in the things which you have learned and been assured of, knowing from whom you have learned them.
2 TIMOTHY 3:13-14

CHAPTER
THREE

Who Is Our Enemy and Why Does He Hate Us?

Don't think for a moment that just because you are a good person and have never robbed a bank or murdered anyone that you don't have an enemy. Don't believe that because you have always paid your bills, given to charities at Christmas, and been kind to people in the street that you don't have an enemy. Don't assume that because you set aside special times to think good thoughts about everyone on earth that you don't have an enemy. Don't even hope that being a Christian who goes to church every Sunday and puts money in the offering basket without even so much as a whimper means that you don't have an enemy. You do. And if you don't realize it, then your enemy has you right where he wants you. He can go completely undetected while he works freely to destroy your life.

Right now we are battling an enemy of whom we are very much aware, because we can see the effects of his works of terror and evil all over the world. But we have an enemy at a deeper, spiritual level, too. He is like a terrorist to our soul. He works undercover, prowling around, planning ways to bring fear, destruction, and death to our lives. We must battle him, not with missiles, tanks, and bomber planes, but with prayer, praise, and the Word of God. Let me tell you some important things you should know about him.

Our enemy is against God and His people. Satan has been our enemy from the beginning. He was there in the Garden of Eden drawing Adam and Eve away from God by causing them to doubt God's word and enticing them to disobey God's laws. He still does that today. That's why people (or nations) who stand for godly virtues like righteousness, peace, love, compassion, and goodness will be hated by all those who follow Satan. And it will always be that way because there is no end to how many people are willing to believe the devil's lies and serve him when he appeals to their fleshly desires. Men who declare themselves to be our enemies may try to legitimize their brand of evil by disguising it as a religion or a cause or an organization of some sort, but it will soon become evident that they are against God, His people, and His ways. Just examine the fruit of their lives, and you will see their true colors revealed.

Our enemy hates us because of who we are. We don't like it when people don't love us. But we can't make our enemy like us unless we become like him. "Those also who render evil for good, they are my adversaries, because I follow what is good" (Psalm 38:20). The enemy will never love us because that would be opposed to all that he stands for. We stand for justice. He promotes injustice. We stand for individual rights and freedom. He is against both. We stand for the liberty to worship God the way we choose. He says we can only worship who and how *he* chooses. We say that every person has value. He says that no life has value unless it is serving his desire. We stand for helping the weak and defenseless. He attacks and destroys them. Satan and the people who follow him hate anyone who doesn't worship him and align with his ways. So it doesn't matter how hard we try to make our enemy like us, he will always be our enemy.

Our enemy is a deceiver. The Bible says of the devil, "He was a murderer from the beginning, and does not stand in the truth, because there is no truth in him. When he speaks a lie, he speaks from his own resources, for he is a liar and the father of it" (John 8:44). There are people all over the world struggling with the devil, and many are actively serving him. But most of them don't even know it. They are being deceived because they can't identify him. They have built their entire lives on a lie without realizing it. But we know who the devil is and can "resist him, steadfast in the faith, knowing that the same sufferings are experienced by your brotherhood in the world" (1 Peter 5:9). We can pray for a breaking down of this stronghold of blindness and deception that he has erected around people's minds.

Our enemy manifests as different people at different times. The men who are our enemies today may be gone next week, next month, or next year, but there will be new names and faces to take their place. That's because Satan will always find bloodthirsty men filled with pride and a lust for power who are willing to believe his lies and do his bidding to try and destroy the people of God. King David said of his enemies, "they are ever with me" (Psalm 119:98). So getting rid of one enemy doesn't mean the battle is over and we can stop praying. We must continue to stand strong against the powers of darkness and be united against the perpetrators of evil. The Bible says, "We do not wrestle against flesh and blood, but against principalities, against powers, against the rulers of the darkness of this age, against spiritual hosts of wickedness in the heavenly places" (Ephesians 6:12). That doesn't mean we never go to war with people. It just means that the battle begins in prayer long before we take action on the battlefield.

Our enemy comes to rob and murder. "The thief does not come except to steal, and to kill, and to destroy. I have come

that they may have life, and that they may have it more abundantly" (John 10:10). When we see men whose goal in life is
to murder, rob, and bring destruction on everything that is
decent and good, we can be certain who their God is. God
gives us a place to hide from an enemy like this. We can hide
ourselves in the Lord for protection. "A prudent man foresees
evil and hides himself; the simple pass on and are punished"
(Proverbs 27:12). Prayer is the means by which that can
happen. Those of us who serve the Lord know that "evil men
do not understand justice, but those who seek the LORD understand all" (Proverbs 28:5). Whenever you see a group of people
who are opposed to the ways of God, you can be certain that
they are serving the purposes of our enemy, the devil, and they
are without true understanding.

Our enemy is not as powerful as he wants us to believe.
Satan is not even close to being as powerful as God is, but he
wants us to think he is. And he will overpower anyone who
doesn't understand that. Because of what Jesus accomplished
on the cross, the devil is a defeated foe. He can't take our life
and do what he wants with it unless we allow him to. He can't
have our soul unless we give it to him. He can only accomplish
what he does through lies and deception. It's our responsibility
to recognize his lies and expose them for what they are. We do
that by standing on the ultimate truth, which is the Word of
God. The Word of God says that we have been given authority
"over all the power of the enemy" (Luke 10:19). But so often
we let the enemy get away with too much because we don't
exercise our God-given authority to control his access to our
lives.

Our enemy never takes a vacation. Satan never has a
benevolent day, so we shouldn't make the mistake of thinking
that our enemy has a day when he is feeling generous toward
us. Don't believe for a moment that there is a limit to the
destruction he wants to bring upon our lives. "Hell and
destruction are never full" (Proverbs 27:20). Our enemy never
takes a day off from doing evil, so that's why we can't let down

our prayer guard. The Bible says, "Be sober, be vigilant; because your adversary the devil walks about like a roaring lion, seeking whom he may devour" (1 Peter 5:8). We must take our praying seriously and not let down our guard.

Our enemy will always overplay his hand. Satan consistently pushes his cause to the limit. But whenever he does, it plays right into God's hand. He thought he had really won when Jesus was crucified. But that sealed his fate. The evil men who planned and participated in bringing down the towers of the World Trade Center and the walls of the Pentagon thought they had really accomplished something. But it sealed their fate. Their destruction is certain and their eternal future will be far worse than anything they hoped to bring upon the thousands of innocent people they destroyed on earth. Instead of destroying our country, it made us stronger. Instead of scattering the people of God, it brought us together to pray in greater power than ever before.

Our enemy can be resisted. Even though evil men work to destroy us, our ultimate enemy is the devil. God says that when we resist him, he will flee from us. As we expose his methods and his lies, refuse to align with him in our actions and words, and take proper authority over him as we pray for his plans to be defeated, the Holy Spirit gives us strength to resist Him. "Those who forsake the law praise the wicked, but such as keep the law contend with them" (Proverbs 28:4). We can pray that the devil working in our enemy will have no power. God promises that "when the wicked are multiplied, transgression increases; but the righteous will see their fall" (Proverbs 29:16). The people who keep God's laws and stand against the devil can predict the downfall of the wicked.

Our enemy is no match for our Savior. Just because we have a full-time enemy does not mean we need to focus on him. We don't. He is nothing. Jesus is everything. Our focus should be on the Lord. The Bible says, "Be wise in what is good, and simple concerning evil" (Romans 16:19). That means we should learn all we can about the Lord and His ways, and just be aware of the truth when it comes to the devil. Jesus came so that "we should be saved from our enemies and from the hand of all who hate us" (Luke 1:71). It is He who defeated Satan so that "we, being delivered from the hand of our enemies, might serve Him without fear, in holiness and righteousness before Him all the days of our life" (Luke 1:74-75). Your focus should be to live a holy and righteous life before the Lord, and trust that "the God of peace will crush Satan under your feet shortly" (Romans 16:20).

Prayer Power

Lord, I thank You that when we live Your way You will not let our enemies triumph over us. Your Word says You will deliver us from those who rise up against us. I pray that You would set us free from the violent men (Psalm 18:48). Show us Your ways, O Lord, so that we may follow You and not fall into the path of the enemy.

Keep me undeceived so that I can always recognize the work of the evil one. Help me to clearly identify who is my enemy and who is not my enemy. "Lead me, O LORD, in Your righteousness because of my enemies; make Your way straight before my face" (Psalm 5:8). Give me Your clear direction. As for my enemies I "pronounce them guilty, O God! Let them fall by their own counsels; cast them out in the multitude of their transgressions, for they have rebelled against You. But let all those rejoice who put their trust in You; let them ever shout for joy, because You defend them; let those also who love Your name be joyful in You. For You, O LORD, will bless the righteous; with favor You will surround him as with a shield" (Psalm 5:10-12).

Help us as a nation to be undeceived. Enable us to spot the enemy even when he is among us and disguised as one of us. Give us discernment to recognize his evil spirit so that we will clearly know who he is. I pray that we will not fall into the trap of being intimidated by our enemy, but will always keep in mind that Your power is far greater than his. Enable us to resist the devil, and thereby resist our enemies, so they will flee from us. Help us to keep our eyes on You, because You are our defender, and You save the upright in heart. I have seen the wicked bring forth iniquity. He thinks up trouble and he proclaims lies. I pray that he will fall into the pit that he has made. May he be caught in his own trap and may his trouble return upon his own head (Psalm 7:14-16). Lord, "let the wickedness of the wicked come to an end, but establish the just" (Psalm 7:9).

Even though our enemies are vigorous and strong and those who hate us wrongfully are many, I know that You, Lord, are stronger. And greater are You who are in us than he who is in the world. Make us wiser than our enemies (Psalm 119:98). O Lord our God, in You we put our trust; save us from all those who persecute us; and deliver us (Psalm 7:1). In Jesus' name I pray.

WEAPONS OF WARFARE

When I cry out to You, then my enemies will turn back;
this I know, because God is for me.
PSALM 56:9

Let God arise, let His enemies be scattered;
let those also who hate Him flee before Him.
PSALM 68:1

By this I know that You are well pleased with me,
because my enemy does not triumph over me.
PSALM 41:11

Depart from me, all you workers of iniquity;
for the LORD has heard the voice of my weeping. The LORD
has heard my supplication; the LORD will receive my prayer.
Let all my enemies be ashamed and greatly troubled.
PSALM 6:8-10

It is God who avenges me, and subdues the peoples
under me; He delivers me from my enemies.
You also lift me up above those who rise against me;
You have delivered me from the violent man.
PSALM 18:47-48

CHAPTER
FOUR

Finding Relief
from Fear and Grief

The ultimate goal of the enemy is our death and destruction. But while he is waiting to accomplish those goals, the two things he likes most to torment us with are fear and grief. There is no shame in having either fear or grief. There is far too much to be afraid of and grieve over in this world. However, it's what we do with both of these emotions that will determine the quality of life we will live. When fear and grief become a controlling factor in our lives, the enemy has us where he wants us. That kind of fear makes us afraid for our future. That kind of grief keeps us locked up in the past.

Not all fear is bad. For example, fear of what *might* happen will keep you from allowing your child to run across a busy highway where there are cars speeding by. It will cause you to lock the doors of your home before you go to bed. It will stop you from playing with a loaded gun. This is *good* fear.

When my children were small, we moved into a house that had a swimming pool in the backyard. I feared that one of them would fall in the pool and drown. This fear caused me to pray every day that God would protect each child and give them a healthy sense of danger. It spurred me to install a high wrought iron fence around the pool with a big padlock on the gate. It inspired me to threaten anyone who might accidentally leave the gate unlocked. It motivated me to give the children swimming lessons until I was confident they were excellent swimmers. As a result, I didn't have to lie awake nights worrying that something bad might happen. I didn't have to live in fear or be gripped by it. Good fear will cause us to do positive and productive things.

Having fear is not wrong. It's when we harbor it and entertain it and let it grow in us that it becomes a problem. That kind of fear overtakes us and controls us and is not of God. It is a spirit of fear. "God has not given us a spirit of fear, but of power and of love and of a sound mind" (2 Timothy 1:7). When we take our fear to the Lord in prayer, He will lift the burden of it by the *power* of His Spirit. He will free us from the torment of it by surrounding us with His *love*. He will keep our mind *sound* and give us peace.

In many nations around the world, the threat of terrorism and crime is all too real. We've seen the damage it can do, and we are right to be afraid of it. But we can't allow our fear to paralyze us. We can't let it rule our lives and disturb our sleeping hours. We can't permit it to become a feeling we live with day after day. That gives our enemies too much power. God has a better quality of life in mind for us. If we draw close to Him, He will help us see what we fear from *His* perspective.

When the servant of the prophet Elisha saw that there was a great enemy army surrounding the city where they were, he was frightened and asked Elisha what they should do about it. Elisha answered him saying, "Do not fear, for those who are with us are more than those who are with them...LORD, I pray, open his eyes that he may see."

Then the Lord opened the servant's eyes, and he saw that "the mountain was full of horses and chariots of fire all around Elisha" (2 Kings 6:15-17). God revealed to Elisha's servant the true reality of his situation.

We, too, can ask God to reveal things to us when we become afraid of all that threatens our safety and peace. When we do, He will give us a keen awareness of His protective presence in our lives. He will instill in our souls a greater knowledge of His power and we'll gain an increased sense of security. Seeing our situation from God's perspective—which is the *true reality*—can free us from fear. But this can *only* happen when we walk close to the Lord and pray.

God also wants us to trust Him enough to take steps of faith in the face of all that we fear. When Pharaoh chased the Israelites to the Red Sea, they were terrified because they were facing an enormous body of water in front of them and Pharaoh's army was fast approaching from behind. They saw no way out. But Moses said to the people, "Do not be afraid. Stand still, and see the salvation of the LORD, which He will accomplish for you today. For the Egyptians whom you see today, you shall see again no more forever. The LORD will fight for you, and you shall hold your peace" (Exodus 14:13-14).

God did all He promised to do. He helped His people by obstructing the sight of the Egyptians with clouds and darkness. He gave the Israelites light at night so they could see. He caused the Red Sea to part so they could walk across on dry land. Of course, the Israelites had to trust God and be courageous enough to walk on the sea floor with a wall of water on either side of them. But they knew they couldn't get to a place of safety and find freedom from fear until they took those steps of faith.

God says that when we are trapped by fear and see no way out, we can call upon Him and He will blind our enemy with darkness. At the same time, He will surround *us* with light. Then we can see the way to go and take the steps necessary to get there. Too often, however, we don't "fight the good fight of faith" in prayer (1 Timothy 6:12). And we don't take the steps of faith God is asking us to take because of our unbelief. We doubt that God hears our prayers and we doubt that He really will protect us.

Unbelief stifles the miraculous things that God wants to do in our lives. Even Jesus Himself could do no miracles in Nazareth because of the people's unbelief. "He could do no mighty work there, except that He laid His hands on a few sick people and healed them. And He marveled because of their unbelief" (Mark 6:5-6). It wasn't *Jesus'* faith that was lacking. It was the *people* who lacked faith. God requires *our* faith in order to accomplish miracles on earth.

Too often, when God doesn't answer our prayers right away, we lose faith that He will answer them at all. But we have to trust His timing. When the prophet Daniel prayed to God, an angel was sent right away to help him. However, it took the angel 21 days to get through to him because he had to fight strong enemy opposition in the spirit realm (Daniel 10:12-13). We need to keep in mind that when we pray there is a spiritual battle that takes place in the invisible realm. How many times have we stopped praying just short of seeing God answer because we became discouraged or doubtful when we had to wait?

It's hard to have faith in the midst of frightening circumstances, but the Bible promises if you have faith, "nothing will be impossible for you" (Matthew 17:20). "Whatever things you ask when you pray, believe that you receive them, and you will have them" (Mark 11:24). But you have to "ask in faith, with no doubting, for he who doubts is like a wave of the sea driven and tossed by the wind. For let not that man suppose that he will receive anything from the Lord" (James 1:6-7). Faith in God's power and love is of utmost importance in overcoming fear. Whenever you are afraid, ask yourself the following two questions:

1. *Do I believe God is powerful enough to protect me?*

2. *Do I believe God loves me enough to care what happens to me?*

If you answered no to either of these questions, ask God to show you the truth you have missed and increase your faith in the process.

If *fear* is the way our enemy keeps us from moving success-fully into the *future* God has for us, then *grief* is the way he will keep us from moving out of the *past* and on with our lives.

Everyone in the world experiences grief at one time or another. And too often an entire nation will experience a col-lective grief over a national tragedy. But that grief can be par-alyzing. I am not saying for a moment that we shouldn't grieve. We absolutely must. If we do not grieve over the losses we experience and the terrible things we witness, we live in denial. We need to go through every stage of grief in order to get to the other side of it. But if we don't walk with God through it, we can't receive the total healing He has for us. That's why we must pray for the people of our country to be healed of their grief, past and present. Healing from grief doesn't mean that we won't ever again feel the loss. It means that we won't become so gripped by the loss that we never get over its torment.

King David suffered a great deal of grief in his lifetime because of his enemies. "I am weary with my groaning; all night I make my bed swim; I drench my couch with my tears. My eye wastes away because of grief; it grows old because of all my enemies" (Psalm 6:6-7). But when David cried out to the Lord, God comforted him. We don't want to waste away and grow old before our time because of our grief. We don't want to become weary or chronically depressed. It's better to call out to the Lord so we can know His comfort. But so often we don't cry out.

When my best friend died of cancer, my grief was so great that I thought I would never get over the loss. She had been my closest friend for 28 years. Even well over a year after her death, I still couldn't shake the grip of sadness that I felt every day. Some days it was nearly incapacitating. I was so aware of the need to go through the different stages of grief that I didn't even think to ask to be delivered of it. I thought it was just something that time would take care of.

When time didn't take care of it, and I couldn't get rid of the sadness, I finally shared the depth of what I was feeling with my prayer partners. Although they had prayed for me regarding this in the past, on this particular morning they recognized that I was struggling with a spirit of grief that was controlling my life. When they prayed for that grief to be broken and for me to be free of it, I felt that feeling lift completely. It wasn't that I never again felt the loss, or that I didn't miss my friend anymore, but now I could enjoy the memory of her without always feeling the pain.

I share this story with you because there was a particular moment in time when I know that the grip of grief was broken in my soul, and a healing balm filled the empty place in my heart. Only God can do that. And only when we pray. But too often we don't pray about such things. Too often we live with more sorrow than we can bear. But God doesn't want that for us. He wants us to draw close to Him in our time of loss, so we can know the joy that can *only* be found in *His presence.*

Many people in my country and your country and all over the world are suffering right now with overwhelming fear and grief to the point of despair. Our prayers of faith for them can help lift that anguish. In doing so we "bear one another's burdens, and so fulfill the law of Christ" (Galatians 6:2). Bearing the burdens of other people doesn't mean that we suddenly have their fear and grief and *they don't.* It means that we ask Jesus to lift their fear and grief and *He does.* The burden we bear is in the actual praying. This doesn't mean they won't *go* through stages of grief. It means that they will *get* through them and experience the awesome gift of God's restoration.

The power of people praying for us when we are struggling with fear and grief should never be underestimated. Nor should the power of *our* prayers for *others.* Prayer can make the difference in whether we, or the people we care about, find healing from fear and grief or remain in the grip of it for the rest of our lives.

Prayer Power

Lord, just as You opened the eyes of Elisha's servant when he prayed and then he could see the mountains full of horses and chariots of fire all around them, I pray You would open our spiritual eyes to see Your hand of protection in our lives when we look to You. Hear us when we call, O God of our righteousness! Relieve us in our distress; have mercy on us, and hear our prayers (Psalm 4:1). Lord, I know that You did not create us to live in fear. I see that the source of all we are afraid of in the world comes from Satan, our enemy. It is *his* doing when we live in fear.

I pray that You would take away the things that give us good reason to be frightened. Remove crime from our streets and criminals from our midst. Expose all criminal activity and cause the plans of the enemy to fail. I pray that all evildoers will be brought to utter confusion, even before their plans are attempted. We cry out to You as a nation to bring all perpetrators to justice. Give us safe streets, safe homes, safe places to work, and safety when we travel. Take away all my fear, Lord. You are "my light and my salvation; whom shall I fear?" You are "the strength of my life; of whom shall I be afraid?" I pray that "though an army may encamp against me, my heart shall not fear" (Psalm 27:1,3).

Lord, for people all over my country who are suffering with fear, I pray that You would reveal Yourself to them and replace their fear with Your perfect love. Help them to know Your delivering power. Give them full knowledge of Your presence. Enable those of us who believe in You to have stronger faith than we have ever had before. I pray that "those who know Your name will put their trust in You; for You, LORD, have not forsaken those who seek You" (Psalm 9:10). Give us peace. Help us to not "fret because of him who prospers in his way, because of the man who brings wicked schemes to pass." I know that "evildoers shall be cut off, but those who wait on the LORD, they shall inherit the earth" (Psalm 37:7-9). Give Your angels charge over us to keep us in all our ways (Psalm 91:11).

I know Your delivering power is the only thing that can free us from the torment of fear and completely restore us. I pray for the promise of that to be fulfilled in me and in each person who cries out to You in their suffering today. Help us to wait on You and be of good courage so You can strengthen our hearts (Psalm 27:14). For I know that "those who wait on the LORD shall renew their strength; they shall mount up with wings like eagles, they shall run and not be weary, they shall walk and not faint" (Isaiah 40:31).

For those who are suffering with grief today, I pray that You would surround each one with Your love. Where I have grief in my soul for any loss I have suffered, I surrender it to You. Help me at the appropriate time to be delivered from that grief so that I can move into the future You have for me. Fill that empty place in my heart and soul with Your healing love. Help me to walk through each day with You, knowing You have promised in Your Word that my time of mourning will end (Isaiah 60:20). In Jesus' name I pray.

WEAPONS OF WARFARE

The Spirit of the Lord GOD is upon Me,
because the LORD has anointed Me to preach
good tidings to the poor; He has sent Me to heal
the brokenhearted, to proclaim liberty to the captives,
and the opening of the prison to those who are bound;
to proclaim the acceptable year of the LORD, and the day of
vengeance of our God; to comfort all who mourn,
to console those who mourn in Zion, to give them beauty
for ashes, the oil of joy for mourning, the garment of
praise for the spirit of heaviness; that they may be called
trees of righteousness, the planting of the LORD, that He may
be glorified. And they shall rebuild the old ruins, they shall
raise up the former desolations, and they shall repair the
ruined cities, the desolations of many generations.
ISAIAH 61:1-4

I have heard your prayer, I have seen your tears;
surely I will heal you.
2 KINGS 20:5

Peace I leave with you, My peace I give to you;
not as the world gives do I give to you.
Let not your heart be troubled, neither let it be afraid.
JOHN 14:27

I cried to the LORD with my voice, and He heard me
from His holy hill. I lay down and slept;
I awoke, for the LORD sustained me.
PSALM 3:4-5

Now faith is the substance of things hoped for,
the evidence of things not seen.
HEBREWS 11:1

CHAPTER
FIVE

The Power of a
Praying Nation

When I homeschooled my daughter her last two years of high school, one of our greatest memories was studying American history together. I say "together" because I felt like a student all over again. I had always liked history, but this time around, because I wanted to impart a love for American history to her, I got into it more than I ever had in the past. It came alive to me as I put myself in the scenes of the brave men and women who discovered, settled, and established this land.

My daughter and husband and I even went on a field trip to Plymouth, Massachusetts, to see a replica of the *Mayflower*, the first boat to bring the Pilgrims to America. As I looked at that little, cramped, fragile boat I tried to figure out how in the world they could sail clear across the Atlantic Ocean safely in it. I decided it was impossible. Another thing that seemed impossible was their surviving in a place where there were no grocery stores, hospitals, doctors, drugstores, or anything at all with which to start a life and a community. I thought they either must have had a death wish or they were lunatics. Or they were led by the Lord to go there. In that moment, looking at that boat, I knew it was the Lord.

That might not seem like a great revelation to some people, but to me it made all of American history make sense. And I saw that there were important key elements about our early history that had been left out of my history books when I was in school. As I did some research and found a number of great books that told the whole truth about what really happened, I realized that our nation was founded on prayer.

Christopher Columbus, who discovered America in 1492, was a strong believer who wanted God to use him to proclaim the Lord's name on the earth. In the only book Christopher Columbus wrote, called *Book of Prophecies*, he said he could not have reached the shores of America without prayer and the guidance of the Holy Spirit.

In his own words he stated, "It was the Lord who put it into my mind....I could feel His hand upon me...the fact that it would be possible to sail from here to the Indies....All who heard of my project rejected it with laughter, ridiculing me....There is no question that the inspiration was from the Holy Spirit....I did not make use of intelligence, mathematics, or maps....No one should fear to undertake a task in the name of our Savior if it is just and the intention is purely for His service."*

Can you imagine that? Christopher Columbus writes that he didn't use a map or any strategic calculations when he sailed to America. He did it with prayer. He traveled clear across the Atlantic Ocean and arrived on our shores with the leading of the Holy Spirit. Can there be any doubt that God wanted him to come here?

Later on, this nation was settled by people of prayer who followed God to a place where He could be worshiped freely without the restrictions of men. The Pilgrims who sailed to America in 1620 felt so passionately about this that they left all that was familiar to them to risk their lives traveling to an

---

* Mark A. Beliles and Stephen K. McDowell, *America's Providential History* (Charlottesville, PA: Providence Press, 1989), p. 45.

unknown and unsettled land in order to be free to live and worship God's way. They had great faith that God would help them find this place and build it. And so He did.

The 102 passengers of that tiny boat sailed 66 days before landing at what is now called Cape Cod. Once they landed they still could all have died in the wilderness. And some of them did not survive the brutal winter. But those who lived prayed fervently to God, and He saved them. They knew without a doubt that God called them, guided them, protected them, and established them.

None of these people stepped into their boat without prayer. And the first thing they did when they landed was to offer thanks to God. They survived this wild untamed land because God enabled them to do so.

As they built homes and communities for themselves, they relied entirely on the Scriptures to teach them God's ways. They homeschooled every child with the main purpose being to teach them to read the Scriptures for themselves. Noah Webster, who wrote the first American dictionary, was a Christian who acknowledged God as the giver of his talent and source of his ability to accomplish such a monumental task.

Every important event in our nation's early history was founded upon a strong faith in God and fervent prayer. For example:

- The men who drew up and signed the Declaration of Independence believed they were establishing America as a Christian nation and relied on God to help them draft this document. Because they wanted it to reflect their faith in God, they specifically stated their belief that "all men are created equal, that they are endowed by their creator with certain unalienable rights."

- During the drawing up of the Constitution, all the men involved found themselves disagreeing on some issues. It seemed that they had reached an impasse. Then Benjamin Franklin, one of our godly leaders, stepped forward to remind the men of all the miracles God had done on their behalf in the past. He said, "The longer I live, the more convincing proofs I see of this truth: that God governs in the affairs of man. And if a sparrow cannot fall to the ground without His notice, is it probable that an empire can not rise without His aid?"* He then called the men to prayer every morning that they were together. After their very first morning of prayer, the air was cleared, and they were able to come to agreement. They created a document that has kept our nation strong for over two hundred years. They were certain they could not have succeeded without guidance from God.

- During our Civil War, President Abraham Lincoln called for a national day of fasting and prayer in order to confess the nation's sins of slavery and pride, and then repent of them. They then acknowledged God's goodness to them and humbly asked for His forgiveness. Within two days after that day of prayer, everything turned around, and it paved the way for victory, the preservation of the Union, and the freeing of the slaves.

There are countless examples throughout the history of our nation when leaders called people to pray in a hopeless situation and saw God completely reverse everything. But these events that illustrate the hand of God as it moved in our nation in response to prayer are not presented as such in our public school textbooks. I had to search them out in Christian history books. You can do that too in whatever country you are in. Even if they are not written up in a book, ask some pastors or Christian leaders in your country for examples of how people have prayed to God on behalf of your nation and have seen answers to their prayers. It will increase your faith and inspire you to pray more for your nation.

* Mark A. Beliles and Stephen K. McDowell, *America's Providential History* (Charlottesville, PA: Providence Press, 1989), p. 172.

God is the same today as He has always been. He says if we will humble ourselves through fasting, confession, and repentance for the sins of our nation, and stop doing our own thing and start living His way, then He will hear our prayers and heal our land (2 Chronicles 7:14). These are words we can't afford to ignore. Only God can help us get rid of evil. Only He can protect us from danger and threats to our safety. Only He can unify us and put us on the right path. But we have to do our part.

You may be saying, "How can I repent for the sins of someone else? That doesn't make sense. Why do I have to repent when I have not done the things that I am confessing? How does that work?" I'm not sure exactly how it works, but I know Jesus did it for you and me. Only He went a giant step further. He bore the price of those sins in Himself. God is not asking us to pay the penalty of our nation's sins. He is asking us to repent of them on behalf of those who don't know how, so that His blessings can be poured out upon us. Sin separates us from God. Confession and repentance removes the separation.

God said to the sinful nations, "Stand in the ways and see, and ask for the old paths, where the good way is, and walk in it; then you will find rest for your souls. But they said, 'We will not walk in it'...therefore hear, you nations...I will certainly bring calamity on this people—the fruit of their thoughts, because they have not heeded My words, nor My law, but rejected it" (Jeremiah 6:16-19).

This is a prediction for any nation who forsakes God and His ways. I know that you and I and millions of believers have not forsaken God and His ways, but others in our nation have. And God gives us a way to eliminate the ramifications of that by confessing the sins of the nation before Him and asking Him to heal our land. He didn't say that all people in a nation must be perfect in their heart and actions in order to receive the blessings of God. If that were the case, there would never be a nation that was blessed. God allows us, who are called by His name, to humble ourselves and repent for the sins of others so that we can receive the blessings He has for us. It's God's gift to us so that we don't have to keep paying the price for the sin of unrepentant people.

In ancient biblical history, time and time again when Israel served the Lord and did what was right in God's sight, the Lord blessed them. But when they became disobedient to God's ways or worshiped idols instead of God, their enemies ran over them, took them captive, killed them, and brought destruction on their land.

When David was a young boy, he faced the giant Goliath boldly declaring, "the battle is the LORD'S, and He will give you into our hands" (1 Samuel 17:47). And that was exactly what God did. David faced a foe far greater than himself, but God won the battle for him. When David became king, Israel won battles not because of how many soldiers they had, nor with the brilliance of their strategists on the battlefield. They won because the Lord went to battle with them.

Even so, King David in his later years, after having won so many battles with the help of God, foolishly decided to take a census to find out exactly how many "valiant men who drew the sword" there were in his army (2 Samuel 24). He wasn't trying to find out the number of soldiers for a particular battle he was facing. He wanted to know exactly how mighty his army was. And he did this just after praising God because "the LORD had delivered him from the hand of all his enemies" (2 Samuel 22:1).

Although David wasn't a perfect man, he did have a heart for God and was immediately convicted about what he had done. He realized that he could not claim strength to win a war on the basis of how many soldiers he had. His victories had always been on God's terms and on the basis of God's power. But even though David repented of his transgression, there was still a price to pay. God sent the prophet Gad to David to give him three choices as a punishment. He could choose either seven years of famine, or running from his enemy for three months, or three days of plague in his nation.

David's response was, "Please let us fall into the hand of the LORD, for His mercies are great; but do not let me fall into the hand of man" (2 Samuel 24:14). So he chose the three days of plague, and as a result 70,000 of his men died. He ended up losing a large portion of the same army he had so proudly numbered.

Gad then instructed David to erect an altar to God in order to give an offering to Him. David chose to *buy* the threshing floor where it was to be done instead of just borrowing it because he said he would not offer to God that which cost him nothing. David then prayed for the people, and God withdrew the plague (2 Samuel 24:21-25). What happened to David happens to a lot of us—especially as we get older. We take for granted the blessings and answers to prayer that we enjoy and begin to think it's because of something *we* have done.

All over the world there are nations facing a foe that appears enormous. But if we ask God to fight our battle for us, we will win. "Blessed is the nation whose God is the LORD, the people He has chosen as His own inheritance" (Psalm 33:12). A people who worship God and proclaim Him to be their Lord will have His blessings. A people who choose to do things their own way instead of relying on God and *His* power will experience disaster.

But God requires a sacrifice on our part. Our prayers are a sacrifice of time and inconvenience. Fasting is a sacrifice of discomfort and self-denial. Repentance is a sacrifice of pride and self-serving. Giving is a sacrifice of something we have. When we make a sacrifice that costs us something, we will see the mighty hand of God move on our behalf.

How do we get an entire nation to pray in unity? We probably can't. That's because there will always be people who oppose God and His ways in any nation. But we don't have to worry about that, because the believers in a nation can join together and repent and pray on behalf of all the people and God will answer. Fortunately, we don't all have to be in the same room at the same time. We can be in our individual prayer closets or houses of prayer and worship. As long as we pray in unity, God's power will be in attendance.

In America, prayer is one of the freedoms protected by our Constitution. We have enjoyed so many blessings as a nation because from the beginning there were believers who prayed. We have no idea how many terrible things we may have avoided because of fervent prayer. If we want a glimpse of what our nation might be like if there were no one praying, all we need to do is look at the conditions in some of the nations who have rejected God completely.

The power of evil in our world today threatens our safety, peace, and freedom. But God still leads us, and His power is always greater. Our world may be shaken, but the kingdom of God is not. We are moving into a new time and there are sacrifices that need to be made. But with the leading of the Lord and the prayers of the believers, we can make them.

Let's serve the Lord as soldiers of His praying army. Let's not live in fear of what man can do to us; rather, let us fear what life would be like without God on our side. Now more than ever we need to heed God's call to prayer. We know too much not to do so. Let's rise up and become strong in prayer so we can see the power of God released to work on earth in a greater way than ever before.

Prayer Power

Lord, I thank You for the men and women of God all over the world who have covered our nation in prayer. I know there are countless blessings which we enjoy because of their faithfulness to You. May those prayers increase until a revival of faith breaks out all across our land.

I pray that no evil will befall our nation and no plague will come near us. Make us immune so we will "not be afraid of the terror by night...nor the pestilence that walks in the darkness" (Psalm 91:5-6). Protect us from the enemy who would like to destroy us. Render his weapons useless. Be with us to deliver us in our time of trouble, give us long life, and show us Your salvation. Deliver us from the snare of the fowler and from the perilous pestilence (Psalm 91:3). Lift us above the things that threaten us. Cover us as we take refuge in You.

Lord, I thank You for all the believers in our nation who serve and glorify You. Thank You for their many prayers and for the answers that You have given. Give us repentant hearts as we humble ourselves before You and turn from our selfish ways. As a nation we confess any pride and lack of faith. Open our blind eyes to see You and Your truth as we seek Your face.

I know that the power of a praying nation is *Your* power working on behalf of those who pray. And I know that when we call upon You, You will answer. I ask this day that You would pour out Your Spirit on every city, town, community, school, government office, business, and church in this country. Reveal

Yourself to people everywhere so that their eyes will be opened to Your truth. Help us to become the praying nation You want us to be. In Jesus' name I pray.

WEAPONS OF WARFARE

He has made from one blood every nation of men
to dwell on all the face of the earth, and has determined
their preappointed times and the boundaries of their
dwellings, so that they should seek the Lord,
in the hope that they might grope for Him and find Him,
though He is not far from each one of us.
ACTS 17:26-27

Therefore, since we are receiving a kingdom which cannot
be shaken, let us have grace, by which we may serve God
acceptably with reverence and godly fear.
HEBREWS 12:28

By swearing and lying, killing and stealing and
committing adultery, they break all restraint, with bloodshed
upon bloodshed. Therefore the land will mourn.
HOSEA 4:2-3

My people are destroyed for lack of knowledge.
HOSEA 4:6

You will hear of wars and rumors of wars.
See that you are not troubled; for all these things
must come to pass, but the end is not yet.
For nation will rise against nation, and kingdom
against kingdom. And there will be famines, pestilences,

and earthquakes in various places. All these are
the beginning of sorrows...but he who endures
to the end shall be saved.

MATTHEW 24:6-8,13

CHAPTER
SIX

Where Do I Go
to Join God's Army?

Years ago when the United States was trying to get people to enlist in the armed forces they put up signs everywhere that said, "Uncle Sam Wants *You!*" In this particular advertisement the United States government was personified as a tall thin man with a white beard wearing red-and-white striped trousers, a blue coat with tails, and a star-studded top hat, and his name was Uncle Sam. (His initials, of course, were U.S.) Those signs were effective because they made the request to join the army very personal and friendly.

Today *you* are being called to become part of an army too. It's a *spiritual army* and it is the most powerful and effective army in existence. That's because the Commander-in-Chief is God Himself, who is all-knowing and invincible and can mobilize His army in a moment's notice. What this army can accomplish is nothing less than miraculous. The goal of the army is to protect the nation from enemy assault, and move it forward into the will of God. It's a goal we *can't* attain without

God. And it's something God *won't* do without *us*. In other words, Father God Wants *You!*

When you fight in this army, you will not be fighting in the flesh. "For though we walk in the flesh, we do not war according to the flesh. For the weapons of our warfare are not carnal but mighty in God for pulling down strongholds" (2 Corinthians 10:3-4). This means that this army of millions, who are spread all over the world, moves entirely as they are led by the Holy Spirit.

One of the great things about this army is that the battlefield is wherever you are. You can go to war in your own prayer closet, living room, car, workplace, backyard, or church. You can do your part alone or together with other believers. Preferably both, because praying in greater numbers means greater power. And because God's army is so vast and on constant alert, there are always many people praying at any given time.

The only problem with this army is that sometimes the soldiers don't hear the call. They get busy or distracted with other things. And because some mistakenly think their contribution isn't important enough to make a difference, they neglect to follow orders. Or they believe the enemy's propaganda and become intimidated when he tries to convince them that *his* army is more powerful than God's. This can be discouraging for many a potential soldier, so we seasoned ones must remember to encourage the newer recruits.

God has equipped everyone in this army with the most efficient and unbeatable weapons. The three most important ones are prayer, praise, and the Word of God. Used properly, there is no enemy that can prevail against them. We have other weapons, too. They may appear harmless at first, but actually they can be quite ruthless. One such stealth weapon is love. When directed towards certain targets it can literally melt them. Others weapons, such as purity, righteousness, humility, repentance, obedience, and faith, can dramatically increase the effectiveness of each soldier. That's why it is worth our while to train diligently in each area. One never knows when there may come a day that any one of these will be the absolute weapon of choice for the moment. It could make the difference between a successful maneuver and disaster.

Every soldier fights better when emboldened by determination and resolve. Those two things are best obtained by observing the pain and suffering of others around us. Indignation at what the enemy is doing in people's lives usually moves us to boldness in prayer. That's why *compassion* for people and a *passion* for God are two very important qualifications needed to be a good soldier in this army.

Good soldiers don't wait until the enemy attacks before they start preparing. They know that they are in a war with an enemy who never gives up. They realize the enemy is constantly opposing them, so they are always fortifying themselves in God's Word and working on their ability to praise and worship Him to the fullest. And we can never underestimate the extent to which our enemies will go to see us destroyed. If we were always thinking as big as our enemy, I'm sure we would pray more than we do.

The time for the army to be most alert is when things are going well. Just because we don't see smoke on the battlefield and hear enemy fire doesn't mean we can relax our prayer vigil. We have to be always watchful. Most of us in the United States were not on alert on September 11 until we got the word. Then God's army was mobilized all over the world. Those prayers may have kept more deaths and destruction from happening than surely would have. Those prayers may have enabled thousands of people to get out of buildings and to a place of safety. Those prayers may have enabled godly and heroic men to successfully bring down an airplane before it crashed into another building, possibly killing hundreds more people.

God's army is an all-volunteer army, so we have to enlist. We do that by saying, "Lord, I want to be an important part of Your army of prayer warriors. Teach me how to intercede for my nation and the world. Make me sensitive to the promptings of Your Holy Spirit." Then listen to whatever God puts on your heart. And if the Holy Spirit wakes you in the middle of the night with a heavy burden, don't roll over and go back to sleep. Ask Him to show you what it is and how to pray. If you can't get a clear leading, pray about whatever comes to your mind and heart. It could make the difference between life and death. Even though the results of your prayers are not always evident right away, the moment you pray something is set in motion.

In God's army we never fight alone. That's because He goes with us to fight our battles. God says, "Today you are on the verge of battle with your enemies. Do not let your heart faint, do not be afraid, and do not tremble or be terrified because of them; for the LORD your God is He who goes with you, to fight for you against your enemies, to save you" (Deuteronomy 20:3-4). We do our part by praying, but the battle is the Lord's. Knowing that makes us certain of the outcome.

In this army, we may never be awarded medals or badges, but when we get to heaven there will be a reward far greater than any we could ever receive on earth. And just knowing that we served the King well and the battle was ultimately won will be all the reward we will need.

Prayer Power

Lord, I want to be one of Your faithful people who understands who the enemy is, what the war is all about, and how to do battle in the Spirit. I know that we do not war according to the flesh, but by Your Spirit in prayer we can cast down everything that exalts itself against You (2 Corinthians 10:5). Teach me how to pray so that my prayers become a mighty weapon against the enemy.

Help me to "put on the whole armor of God" so that I "may be able to stand against the wiles of the devil" (Ephesians 6:11). Help me to gird my waist with Your truth and "put on the breastplate of righteousness." Remind me to cover my feet with "the gospel of peace" and help me to raise up "the shield of faith" so that I can quench "the fiery darts of the wicked one." I have put on the "helmet of salvation" and will take up the sword of the Spirit, which is Your Word. Help me to pray in the Spirit with watchfulness and perseverance so that I might make intercession for all of Your people (Ephesians 6:14-18). I want to serve You well as a prayer warrior. Train me so that I will not fail to understand Your leading.

Lord, raise up Your sons and daughters all over the world to be a strong army of intercessors. Give us the strength we need to stand unshakeable in the face of all that opposes us. Gift us with wisdom to make right decisions, and give us the ability to hear Your instructions. May we be on such a constant vigil that we can be mobilized in an instant. Show us how to wage an effective campaign against the enemy to see him defeated.

Enable us to establish and be actively involved in regular corporate prayer meetings so we can agree together to move *offensively* instead of merely dodging enemy fire. Teach us how to boldly advance into enemy territory in prayer and take back what he has stolen from us. In Jesus' name I pray.

WEAPONS OF WARFARE

You therefore must endure hardship as a good soldier
of Jesus Christ. No one engaged in warfare entangles himself
with the affairs of this life, that he may please him who
enlisted him as a soldier.
2 TIMOTHY 2:3-4

When the enemy comes in like a flood,
the Spirit of the LORD will lift up a standard against him.
ISAIAH 59:19

You fight and war. Yet you do not have because you do not
ask. You ask and do not receive, because you ask amiss,
that you may spend it on your pleasures.
JAMES 4:2-3

I have pursued my enemies and destroyed them;
neither did I turn back again till they were destroyed.
And I have destroyed them and wounded them,
so that they could not rise; they have fallen under my feet.
For You have armed me with strength for the battle;
You have subdued under me those who rose against me.
2 SAMUEL 22:38-40

For You are my lamp, O LORD; the LORD shall
enlighten my darkness. For by You I can run against
a troop; by my God I can leap over a wall.
2 SAMUEL 22:29-30

CHAPTER
SEVEN

Ears to Hear the
Watchmen's Warning

A watchman is someone who stands guard over a city, or a building, or a piece of property. His job is to sound the warning alarm whenever he sees the enemy approaching or when he senses impending danger.

Centuries ago every town had watchmen stationed at strategic places. Some were placed on high towers in grain fields or vineyards. From that perspective they could guard the field from animals or from people who would try to pillage the crops. Some watchmen were positioned on towers in pastures where they could watch over the cattle and sheep in order to keep them protected from wild beasts or thieves.

The larger cities had high, thick walls around them so as to protect the people inside from enemy attack. The watchmen stood on top of these walls where they could observe everything and sound the alarm if they saw anyone approaching.

The watch itself was a specific time when the watchman was on duty. There were usually four six-hour watches so that all times of the day and night were covered. The night watches were especially dangerous because the enemy liked to move in the dark. That's why watchmen were most concerned about the night watch and always looked eagerly for morning to come (Psalm 127:1).

The prophets of the Old Testament were thought of as watchmen. "I have set watchmen on your walls, O Jerusalem; they shall never hold their peace day or night" (Isaiah 62:6). They warned the nation's leaders and citizens of God's impending judgment upon them if they did not stop their sinful practices and repent.

God has given us watchmen today, also. They fill a purpose similar to that of the ancient ones long ago. They have been given the ability to see things we can't, so they can warn us of enemy encroachment. They can call us to change our ways when we get off track. These are men and women upon whom God has bestowed gifts of discernment, wisdom, revelation, and prophecy. Some of them are Christian pastors and leaders. Some of them are godly politicians and experts. Some of them may not be believers at all, but God has placed them in strategic places and endowed them with great knowledge and will speak through them if we will listen.

Those whom God gives such responsibility must warn people of impending danger. If they see trouble ahead and don't alert us so that we can pray and do what needs to be done, God will hold them accountable. "If the watchman sees the sword coming and does not blow the trumpet, and the people are not warned, and the sword comes and takes any person from among them, he is taken away in his iniquity; but his blood I will require at the watchman's hand" (Ezekiel 33:6). But if they warn us and we don't listen, we must bear the consequences.

While it's true that we should not be preoccupied with our enemy, we are foolish if we act as though we don't have one. We must always be on the lookout for his tactics and watchful of his methods. And we must look to see who our watchmen are and listen for their call, so the enemy doesn't have the element of surprise. And when the watchmen sound the alarm, we have to respond accordingly.

My husband's family came from Armenia, which was actually the first documented Christian nation. The Armenians were converted to Christianity in A.D. 300. In the early 1900s when they were under Turkish rule, Michael's grandmother, Anna, lived in Armenia with her husband and two daughters. She was a very godly, praying woman.

Anna often told the story about a certain period of time when a number of godly Christian prophets came through their land foretelling of the coming demise of all Armenians by the hands of the Turks. Anna knew in her spirit it was a warning from God, but most people ignored it or took it lightly. These prophetic watchmen called the people to be aware, to pray, and to be ready to defend themselves or leave the country. Even the non-Christians in that area warned them of coming danger. The watchmen had been posted and the trumpet of warning had been sounded. A few people took it seriously and left the country, but most of them did not respond. Anna's husband was one of those who did not respond.

Their lack of willingness to pray and be prepared to escape resulted in 2 million Armenians being slaughtered or chased out of their country when the Turks invaded. Sadly, Anna saw her husband and her two daughters killed in front of her. The young girls were thrown up in the air and caught on the end of a pitchfork. Anna escaped and spent a month hiding in the fields and hills, grazing on nothing but grass, before she was found and rescued. Kind people helped her find passage to New York City. Once she settled in the United States, she married again and had two more daughters, one of which was Michael's mother. Anna was a prayer warrior until the day she died.

God often gives us warnings about things to come. But if our hearts are hard, or if we have turned from His ways to our own, or if we are walking in disobedience, or we choose to live in sin, or are not repentant for sins we have committed in the past, or are too busy to spend time with the Lord in prayer and in His Word, or we fail to reverence God with all that He is due, or we refuse to listen to the warning, then we will not recognize it as such. When our lives are too loud to hear the still small voice as He speaks to us, or when we are too busy to take the time to pay attention, we will suffer the consequences.

In the Old Testament, people laughed at the prophets who warned them of the evil to come and the hand of judgment about to be laid on their nation (2 Chronicles 30:10). Yet the prophets' predictions always came to pass. For years we heard many knowledgeable men warn us that it was only a matter of time before terrorism would strike American soil in a devastating way and that we should be prepared. They were not taken seriously enough and their predictions came to pass. For years we have been told by pastors and godly spiritual leaders that, unless we repent, turn from our own ways, and return to God's ways, there will be serious consequences. God raises up people to be His voice and relay His messages and we are given a certain amount of time to respond. We must pray for ears to hear them.

In many ways we are all called to be watchmen. "What I say to you, I say to all: Watch!" (Mark 13:33-37). But many people wonder if their lone voice can make a difference. And the answer is a resounding "Yes!" There are many examples in the Bible where one person prayed and it changed the course of a nation. When Samuel cried out to the Lord on behalf of Israel as the Philistines attacked them, "the LORD thundered with a loud thunder upon the Philistines that day, and so confused them that they were overcome before Israel" (1 Samuel 7:10). You have no idea how much confusion your prayers can bring upon the enemy of your nation when you watch and pray.

In ancient times the towers that were built for the watchmen to go up into in order to gain a better perspective were very strong and protected. That's why the Lord is referred to in the Bible as a strong tower. "For You have been a shelter for me, a strong tower from the enemy" (Psalm 61:3). The Lord is our strong tower today, too. We can always go to Him in order to find security and gain a clear perspective.

Prayer Power

Lord, I pray that You would make me one of Your watchmen. Show me the things I should see and what I need to know so I can pray the way You want me to. Instruct me when I need to tell others what You have shown me. Help us as a nation to recognize and acknowledge the watchmen You have placed on our walls. Enable us to hear the voices of those who can see more than we can because of their position. Show us how to pray for them and remind us to do so. Help those who know the truth to be able to proclaim it boldly without fear of the criticism of man.

I know that we are no match for the devil without You, Lord, but the devil is certainly no match for You. You are all-powerful. I invite Your power to work in our midst. I realize that unless You guard the city, the watchman stays awake in vain (Psalm 127:1). All our watching is pointless unless You secure and protect us. I declare that You are my strong tower. I run to You to protect me and all I care about from the thief and his plans to steal and destroy. My soul waits for You and in Your Word I put my hope. I wait for You even more than the watchman waits for morning (Psalm 130:6).

Lord, help us to become a praying nation and be able to recognize the signs and warnings we are given. Give us the ability to discern the plans of the enemy before they happen, so we can pray that they will come to nothing. Open our ears to hear when Your watchmen sound the warning. Enable us to understand the message and be diligent to pray as You have commanded us. In Jesus' name I pray.

WEAPONS OF WARFARE

I have made you a watchman for the house of Israel;
therefore you shall hear a word
from My mouth and warn them for Me.
EZEKIEL 33:7

Blessed be the LORD my Rock, who trains my hands for war,
and my fingers for battle—my lovingkindness
and my fortress, my high tower and my deliverer,
my shield and the One in whom I take refuge,
who subdues my people under me.
PSALM 144:1-2

When I bring the sword upon a land, and the people of the
land take a man from their territory and make him their
watchman, when he sees the sword coming upon the land, if
he blows the trumpet and warns the people, then whoever
hears the sound of the trumpet and does not take warning, if
the sword comes and takes him away, his blood shall be on
his own head. He heard the sound of the trumpet, but did
not take warning; his blood shall be upon himself. But he
who takes warning will save his life.
EZEKIEL 33:2-5

I set watchmen over you, saying, "Listen to the sound of the
trumpet!" But they said, "We will not listen."
JEREMIAH 6:17

He who is often rebuked, and hardens his neck, will suddenly
be destroyed, and that without remedy.
PROVERBS 29:1

CHAPTER
EIGHT

Pray for My Enemy?
You've Got to Be Kidding!

I don't know about you, but praying for my enemy is the last thing I think about doing when I've just been attacked. And in the aftermath of the overwhelming death and destruction in our nation caused by terrorists, forgiveness was not even a remote thought in my mind. Surely anyone who chooses to live by the sword and spend their days planning to kill thousands of innocent men, women, and children in the most brutal and ghastly way deserves an eternity in hell, and the sooner it starts the better for all mankind.

But God reminded me that while Jesus was nailed to the cross and dying in agony, He prayed for the men who were crucifying Him saying, "Father, forgive them for they know not what they do" (Luke 23:34). Such amazing forgiveness and love is hard to fathom. Even though Jesus did nothing to deserve His torture and ultimate death, He prayed for the ones who were doing it.

One of the two thieves who were crucified with Him recognized that Jesus had done nothing wrong, while he himself was getting what he deserved for his crime. With a repentant heart the thief asked Jesus to remember him when He came into His kingdom. Jesus, in His ever merciful and compassionate way, promised him, "Today you will be with Me in Paradise" (Luke 23:43).

When I thought about what Jesus did, I realized I needed to get out my "What Would Jesus Do?" bracelet and start wearing it again. I couldn't honestly say that I wanted any of the people who had been responsible for the mass murder in America to be in heaven with me when I got there. And not only was I not inclined to forgive them, but the only prayer I was praying for them was that they would be caught and brought to justice. But God convicted me about my attitude, and I am embarrassed now to admit my temporary lapse of faith in the power of God to transform lives. God reminded me that in His eyes all sin is deserving of death. My sins and your sins are just as deserving of death as a mass murderer's are.

The reason God asks us to forgive and pray for our enemies is not so we can send them daisies and invite them over to roast marshmallows. It's because God hates sin, and unforgiveness is a sin. God says to "love your enemies, bless those who curse you, do good to those who hate you, and pray for those who spitefully use you and persecute you" (Matthew 5:44). He asks us to do that because to do otherwise would be a sin. If we don't love, forgive, and pray for our enemies, there will be no reversal of evil. It will just continue to perpetuate itself. Unforgiveness is what causes the constant fighting year after year in certain parts of the world with one people or group venting their hatred and taking revenge upon another. Without forgiveness, the cycle of hatred never ends.

Also, when we harbor evil in our hearts it puts up a wall between us and God. And it must be a thick wall because it keeps Him from hearing our prayers. "The LORD is far from the wicked, but He hears the prayers of the righteous" (Proverbs 15:29). One of the best reasons to be free of unforgiveness is so that our prayers will not be hindered. Even prayers for our enemy to come to justice must be prayed from a right heart. "Whenever you stand praying, if you have anything against anyone, forgive him, that your Father in heaven may also forgive you your trespasses" (Mark 11:25). If we don't forgive our enemy for his murder, then God doesn't forgive us for our sins, and we don't get our prayers answered as we would like.

Of course in the government of a nation, different sins break different laws and require different punishments. So don't think for a moment that just because a nation has forgiving people in it that they don't go to war with their enemy when they have been viciously attacked. As individuals we must forgive our enemies, but as a nation of law and order, forgiving our enemies doesn't mean letting them off the hook and not making them pay for their crime. Far from it! A nation that allows evil to proliferate violates the laws of God.

God says there is a time for everything. "To everything there is a season, a time for every purpose under heaven...a time of war and a time of peace" (Ecclesiastes 3:1,8). Being viciously attacked by the forces of evil definitely brings about a time for war. When the perpetrators of evil are brought to justice, then it will be a time for peace. God is a God of justice, and He wants the wicked to pay for their crimes. "Though they join forces, the wicked will not go unpunished" (Proverbs 11:21). "I, the LORD, love justice" (Isaiah 61:8).

In the Old Testament, God instructed King Saul to attack Amalek because the Amalekites had ambushed Israel when God brought them out of Egypt. (God doesn't like it when people attack His kids!) The Lord told Saul to "Go, and utterly destroy the sinners, the Amalekites, and fight against them until they are consumed" (1 Samuel 15:18). God specifically instructed Saul to "destroy all they have, and do not spare them" (1 Samuel 15:3). Notice that word *all*.

Saul did attack Amalek the way he was supposed to, but he rebelled against God's instructions and did not destroy *everything*. He instead captured the Amalekite king and the best of the Amalekites' sheep and oxen (1 Samuel 15:21). Saul was punished for that disobedience by eventually losing his throne. His unwillingness to *completely* destroy the enemy meant that the Israelites had to fight them again. If we *don't* destroy evil by bringing it to justice when it attacks, we will most likely be attacked by it again, only next time it could be far worse.

Another reason to forgive our enemy is so he can't continue to hurt us. Unforgiveness and hatred bind us to the one we resent and hate and keep us focused on him. This actually hurts *us* more than it hurts *him*. When you *really* forgive someone, it means that the cruel, unjust, destructive acts they have committed against you lose their ability to destroy you. While our forgiving people who are responsible for evil does not release *them* from their culpability, it does release *us* from *them*. We don't want our own sin of unforgiveness and hatred tying us to them. We want to free ourselves from them so that God can work in their lives. And ours. Always remember that forgiving someone doesn't make that person right. It makes *you free.*

When we forgive people, it doesn't mean they won't have to account for what they have done. They will. If they need to be brought to justice, we can pray for them and commit them to the Lord so He can do that. If they remain unrepentant and steadfastly devoted to evil, if they continue to be set against God and His people, then their future is not bright. The Bible says, "It is a fearful thing to fall into the hands of the living God" (Hebrews 10:31).

God doesn't want us to go after people in order to get revenge. That's *His* job. He says, "Vengeance is Mine, I will repay" (Romans 12:19). He wants us to be led by *Him* when we fight evil. It's better to go to war because we're convicted it is the absolute right thing to do, rather than to get revenge. Besides, our best revenge in the flesh lasts but a moment; God's punishment lasts for eternity. That's why praying for our enemy *is* actually the best revenge. When we pray for someone to have their eyes and heart opened to receive the Lord, often

God will turn their lives upside down and shake out everything they lust after. This means their sinful plans will come to nothing, and their lives will be lived in constant frustration until they get right with God. And the choice will be theirs whether they will turn toward God or suffer the consequences.

The goal should not be to kill people in vengeance. The goal should be to stop evil. In the process of doing that, however, we should not rejoice over our enemy's demise. After the vicious attack upon our nation, international news footage showed people in another country dancing and laughing for joy over the death and destruction of thousands of people in our country. That is exactly what God says not to do. "He who is glad at calamity will not go unpunished" (Proverbs 17:5). If our enemy is destroyed, we can rejoice that God has given us victory. But we are not to laugh at their deaths or dance on their graves.

Let's commit our enemy into the Lord's hands and pray that he will have an encounter with the living God so he can be transformed by the power of the Holy Spirit. How much better than the sweet taste of revenge that turns bitter in our souls, or the reaping of consequences for our own sin, would be the transformation of our enemy into a follower of Christ. What a great way to win a war.

Prayer Power

Lord, Your Word says that "when a man's ways please the LORD, He makes even his enemies to be at peace with him" (Proverbs 16:7). I pray that You would make us to be a people that pleases You so that we can be at peace with our enemies. I know that Satan is an enemy who will never be at peace with us because his ways are opposed to Your ways. And any men who are sold out to Satan's ways will not stop being our enemy until they are free from the grip of Satan. I pray that the enemies of our nation who serve Satan and his purposes will have the blinders taken off of their eyes so they can see Your truth. I pray that they will one day prostrate themselves before You in deep repentance for the sins they have committed. I pray that Jesus will be lifted up to them in such a way that they will be drawn to Him as the source of their life. Even so, whether our enemy responds to Your truth or not, I pray that You will bring him to justice.

I don't want anything to stand in the way of my prayers being answered, so Lord I pray that You would reveal in me any unforgiveness that is in my heart. The persons that I am most needing to forgive are

_____.
I confess my unforgiveness toward them. Help me to forgive them for every offense and crime against me or those whom I care about. I don't want to tie those people to me with my unforgiveness. The acts they committed that are the most hurtful and offensive to me are _____

_____

_____.

I release those offenses into Your hands and ask that You would remove the sting of their memory from my heart so that I can be free of them.

Lord, I don't want my nation to be a people who refuse to live Your way and forsake You, the fountain of living water. I don't want us to do things opposed to Your laws and make our lives to be empty cisterns that hold nothing (Jeremiah 2:13). Help us to live in obedience to Your commandments as a people and a nation. Help us not to go after our enemies out of revenge, but rather enable us to release them into Your hands and then do what is necessary and right to see that justice is done. In Jesus' name I pray.

WEAPONS OF WARFARE

For the eyes of the LORD are on the righteous,
and His ears are open to their prayers; but the face of the
LORD is against those who do evil.
1 PETER 3:12

Open the gates, that the righteous nation that keeps the
truth may enter in. You will keep him in perfect peace,
whose mind is stayed on You, because he trusts in You.
ISAIAH 26:2-3

I have stretched out My hands all day long to a rebellious
people, who walk in a way that is not good,
according to their own thoughts.
ISAIAH 65:2

If we confess our sins, He is faithful and just to
forgive us our sins and to cleanse us from all
unrighteousness. If we say that we have not sinned,
we make Him a liar, and His word is not in us.
1 JOHN 1:9-10

If our heart does not condemn us, we have confidence
toward God. And whatever we ask we receive from Him,
because we keep His commandments and do those things
that are pleasing in His sight.
1 JOHN 3:21-22

CHAPTER
NINE

How Can Good Come from Something So Bad?

On the day of the terrorist attacks upon the United States, our pastor, Rice Broocks, called a special prayer meeting at our church for that evening. Because the congregation is so large, there wasn't time to get in touch with every person individually. So he and other members of the pastoral staff contacted as many people as they could, and from there the news of the meeting spread like wildfire. By seven o'clock that night, the church was packed to overflowing. Everyone who could possibly come on such short notice was there. We all needed to be together as a spiritual family, to draw on God's comfort and strength in worship and praise, and to make a difference by praying for our nation.

The worship time was powerful in a life-changing way, just as worship is meant to be. And afterwards one person after another was asked to come up front to pray about whatever was on their heart regarding the devastating events of that day. We prayed for the nation, our leaders, the victims who might still be alive, the people who had lost loved ones, and for every person who had witnessed those horrifying scenes—especially the children. Each prayer was as powerful and heartfelt as the one before it, making it the most passionate and fervent prayer meeting I have ever attended.

During that evening we felt ourselves gaining much needed strength in our souls. We had all come to church with unbearably heavy hearts, but we walked out with great hope, an absence of fear, a sense of renewed purpose as intercessors, and the joy of the Lord. This wasn't a phony, living-in-denial, pretending-it-didn't-happen kind of mindless joy. It was the joy of knowing that God was still in control in our world and He would somehow bring good out of all that had happened.

That night, Pastor Rice felt a strong leading from the Holy Spirit for him and some of the other pastors and staff from the church to travel to New York City to do whatever they could to help. Throughout the next day they made the necessary arrangements for their trip. That night there was another equally packed and powerful worship and prayer meeting at the church, after which they piled in a van and drove all night from Nashville to New York City. As all the airports in the United States were still closed at that point, driving was the only way to get there.

Once they arrived in New York City, they were struck by the numbers of people who were openly looking to God for answers and spiritual comfort. Although the hospitals stood readily available to take care of wounded bodies, there seemed to also be a great need for hospitals for the wounded of soul.

Recognizing the openness and longing of people's hearts, Pastor Rice knew that the Lord was calling him and the other pastors to plant a church right in the heart of New York City. This is not to say that there weren't many great churches there already, but the need was so enormous, the number of hurting people so great, and the devastation so massive that another strong church in the area seemed essential for bearing the load.

The following Saturday, Pastor Rice and the others drove back to Nashville in time for Sunday services. He shared with the congregation what the Holy Spirit had put on his heart about starting a church in New York City. He shared that they were looking for a suitable place, but that so much property had been destroyed that thousands of others were also looking for buildings in which to relocate their businesses. He said he didn't know where they would find the right place or how to get the thousands of dollars needed, but he knew the Lord would provide it.

Immediately after that service, a gentleman who had been visiting the church that morning came up to Pastor Rice and told him that he had connections with a theatre on Forty-fourth Street off of Broadway. An old historic building called The Lamb's Theatre would be available for their use. The necessary details were put into motion right away and not only was the theater secured, but within that week the many thousands of dollars that were needed had been donated by generous and faithful members of the congregation.

A few weeks later, Morning Star Church New York was born. Immediately it began growing, thriving, birthing new life, and bringing spiritual comfort to many. Every Sunday afternoon after the last morning service at our church in Nashville, Pastor Rice and several members of the pastoral staff and worship team flew to New York City to hold evening services there. Some of them eventually felt led to move there permanently to see this church become an oasis of joy and a beacon of light to people in the area. It all happened with such speed and success that it is now referred to as "The Miracle on Forty-fourth Street."

This is just one example of how something good can come out of the pain of a tragic situation. And only God can accomplish this. But it doesn't just happen. Pastor Rice said,

"There comes a time when we must stop just reading about what we are to do and actually start doing it. The storm that has come upon our culture is not something we should shrink back from, but rather we must realize we are called into the middle of it."

In this instance good came out of something bad because a group of people were eager to seek God and worship Him in the midst of their pain. They were willing to follow the leading of the Holy Spirit, pray fervently, give of themselves, and move into the storm to rescue those who had been overcome by it.

When we experience tragedy and loss, it seems impossible that anything good can come out of it. It may be hard to imagine ever feeling true happiness again. And even though God *promises* that "all things work together for good to those who love God, to those who are called according to His purposes" (Romans 8:28), in disastrous situations we may wonder how in the world God can actually do that for *us*. The truth is He can, no matter how bad our situation. *How* He does it, only *He* knows. But it doesn't happen automatically. There are conditions that have to be met.

Most importantly of all, we must *love God*. If we don't love God, or if we're mad at Him and have an angry, resentful, bitter, unforgiving, or hateful attitude, then this promise will not be fulfilled in our life. God knows what is in our hearts, so we can't hide it from Him. He works all things together for good to those who *love* Him, and He knows if we really love Him or not.

Loving God doesn't mean we just pray when we want something, as if God were a spiritual Santa Claus, a Sugar Daddy, or our fairy Godfather. Of course He *wants* us to ask for things in accordance with His will. In fact, He says we don't have certain blessings because we don't ask for them. But He wants us to love Him enough to not just tell Him what *we* want without asking what *He* wants. In other words, we can't just ignore His laws or reject His ways and then run to Him demanding that He protect us and give us everything we long for. The Bible does *not* say that all things work together for good to those who deny God's existence until disaster strikes and then run to Him and demand that He fix everything that's wrong. That is not loving God.

Loving God is a way of life that does not depend on circumstances. It depends on our knowledge of who God is. When we know who He is, we can't help but love Him. It means trusting Him with all our heart and walking with Him through each day, no matter how difficult it may be. It means always knowing that God is on our side, whether it feels like it at the moment or not. It means praying with the leading of the Holy Spirit and refusing to give in to fear and doubt.

Remember Job in the Bible, the man who did nothing to deserve his fate yet lost everything, including all of his children and his health? Life can't get worse than that. Through it all, however, and even in his greatest hour of grief, he never cursed God (Job 2:3-13). Job knew that bad things happen in life, so when they happened to him, his faith and trust in the goodness of God didn't falter. Job loved God. And because of that, God brought great good out of his suffering by giving him "twice as much as he had before" (Job 42:10). Job enjoyed a good, long life beyond that tragic time, and God blessed his latter days even more than his former ones (Job 42:12).

When the apostle Paul and Silas were beaten and thrown in prison, they didn't curse God because of their plight. Instead, in the middle of the night, they were found "praying and singing hymns to God." As the prisoners were listening to them, "suddenly there was a great earthquake, so that the foundations of the prison were shaken; and immediately all the doors were opened and everyone's chains were loosed" (Acts 16:26). During the difficult time that Paul and Silas were going through, they didn't complain or shake their fists at God and demand to know why He had let them down. Instead, they praised and worshiped Him. Paul and Silas loved God. And as a result, they were set free from their miserable situation.

The most important and powerful way to show love for God is through praise and worship. When we love God, our hearts are filled with thanksgiving for who He is and His awesome and wonderful love for us. Because God inhabits the praises of His people, each time we voice praise and worship to Him, He works powerfully in our midst (Psalm 22:3-4). Through praise and worship we acknowledge His greatness and enthrone Him as King of Kings (Psalm 95:1-5). Through praise and worship we release His power to work in our situation and transform our lives (Psalm 44). Through praise and worship we bring to nothing the devil's plans for our destruction (Psalm 92). Through praise and worship, God keeps us under His covering of protection (Psalm 95:6-7). Through praise and worship, doubt is removed and our faith is increased (Psalm 27).

The most significant thing we can do to see good come out of something bad is to praise and worship God in the midst of it, and then pray as we are led by the Holy Spirit. Things don't just accidentally or coincidentally work out for good. They happen when we draw close to God in worship and praise. This sets the stage for God to move powerfully in response to our prayers. "If anyone is a worshiper of God and does His will, He hears him" (John 9:31).

We also need to ask God to show us what *we* can do to help bring good out of bad situations. Is there something we can plant that will grow into a great blessing for others? Is it a word of hope and comfort to assure people that God loves them and hasn't forsaken them? Is it contributing finances to meet a desperate need? Is it volunteering our time where help is needed? Is it a hand of compassion extended to others? Is it reminding people that no matter how much our world shakes, God is unshakeable? Is it praying with new commitment and dedication? Ask God to show you. And don't be afraid or hesitant if He calls you into the storm. He will be there partnering with you to bring good out of it.

Prayer Power

Lord, I draw close to You and proclaim You to be Lord and King over all heaven and earth. I thank You that Your goodness, mercy, and righteousness endure forever (1 Chronicles 16:34). I praise You according to Your righteousness, and I sing praises to Your name, O Lord Most High (Psalm 7:17). Your name is excellent over all the earth (Psalm 8:1). I praise You for Your mighty acts according to Your excellent greatness (Psalm 150:2). I worship You and I love You, Lord.

May my prayers be set before You as incense, the lifting up of my hands as the evening sacrifice (Psalm 141:2). I give glory to Your name. To You, O Lord, I lift my soul, and the soul of my nation. Let us not be put to shame. Do not permit our enemies to triumph over us (Psalm 25:1-2).

Lord, as the body of Christ we are weary of watching the enemy, whom You defeated on the cross, run roughshod over people and destroy their lives. We are disgusted by our own compromised prayers. We confess that we haven't been willing to lay down enough of our lives to see them break through the darkness with power. Renew us and revive us, Lord. Fill us afresh with Your Holy Spirit. Break down the strongholds in our lives that stand in opposition to You and Your ways. Help us to be doers of the Word and not just hearers only. Work a profound spiritual awakening in Your people all over this land.

Lord, you have said that You are "able to do exceedingly abundantly above all that we ask or think, according to the power that works in us" (Ephesians 3:20). I know that means You can do more than we ever dreamed. I invite You to do that in me, in Your people, and in our country. Ignite a fire in our hearts that illuminates for us the possibilities of what can happen when we pray. Move the hearts in this nation into alignment with Your will.

I ask for Your grace to be poured out upon our nation. Only You can bring good out of any evil that has been manifested here. Show me how I may be of service to You in that regard. Help me not to shrink back when you call me into the storm. Shine Your light into our darkness and evaporate it. Help those of us who believe to extend Your light to others. Thank You, Lord, that You have put gladness in our hearts once again (Psalm 4:7) and are even now making all things work together for good in our nation.

WEAPONS OF WARFARE

You meant evil against me; but God meant it for good,
in order to bring it about as it is this day,
to save many people alive.
GENESIS 50:20

Praise the LORD! I will praise the LORD with my whole heart,
in the assembly of the upright and in the congregation.
The works of the LORD are great, studied by all
who have pleasure in them. His work is honorable
and glorious, and His righteousness endures forever.
He has made His wonderful works to be remembered;
the LORD is gracious and full of compassion.
PSALM 111:1-4

Let the high praises of God be in their mouth,
and a two-edged sword in their hand.
PSALM 149:6

Weeping may endure for a night,
but joy comes in the morning.
PSALM 30:5

Arise, shine; for your light has come! And the glory
of the LORD is risen upon you. For behold, the darkness
shall cover the earth, and deep darkness the people;
but the LORD will arise over you, and His glory
will be seen upon you. The Gentiles shall come
to your light, and kings to the brightness of your rising.
ISAIAH 60:1-3

CHAPTER
TEN

Twelve Ways to Pray for the Heart of My Country

Our world is in a different place now than we have ever been before. Old enemies are now allies. And we have a new enemy whom we can't always see, even though he sometimes dwells among us. He can strike any nation at any time, in any place. We see that our lives can be changed in an instant, even on the most perfect of mornings in the strongest of cities in the safest of buildings or airplanes. Our life, or the lives of those whom we care about, can be taken from us in a moment when evil penetrates our protective barriers. We know we need something greater than ourselves to defeat this enemy. We need the power of God.

Because of that, each of us must make praying for our own nation a habit. The Bible says that in heaven there are "golden bowls full of incense, which are the prayers of the saints," and "the smoke of the incense, with the prayers of the saints" ascends up to God (Revelation 5:8 and 8:4). This says to me that when we pray, our prayers are collected and not thrown away. They are lasting. They don't just come out of our mouth and evaporate into thin air. Our prayers add up so we must do our part to keep those bowls filled.

We must remember to not allow ourselves to fall into prayerlessness when things are going well. We have to keep moving toward the high calling of God in prayer, so that if it comes to a time when our prayers can make the difference between life and death, or the victory of good over evil, we will rise up in the power of God to deliver a defining blow to the enemy *before* he can deliver one to us. Jesus said, "that men always ought to pray and not lose heart" (Luke 18:1). In other words, we must keep praying and not give up.

Rather than suggest specific ways to pray, I have written twelve prayers that will cover the heart and soul of any nation. As you pray these prayers, fill in specific details as you become aware of them. No matter who our enemy is at the moment or what situations we face right now, these prayers will always be relevant.

I hope you will join me in praying these prayers for our respective countries and for the world. Each of us is a link that strengthens and reinforces the chain of prayers that circles the earth and reaches to heaven. God has told us to occupy this earth until He comes. Let's do that. He has asked us to inter-cede for our leaders. Let's obey Him. Let's stop living with a lesser quality of life—a life of fear, danger, or limited free-doms—because we fail to ask God for something better. God says, "I have this day set you over the nations and over the kingdoms, to root out and to pull down, to destroy and to throw down, to build and to plant" (Jeremiah 1:10). Let's join together to see that happen. God is calling you and me to be His instrument of healing, love, deliverance, and salvation, and not only for our nation but for the other nations of the world as well. Let's not let Him down.

Prayer Power

1. Pray for the Leader and His Advisors

Lord, I pray for Your hand of protection to be upon (leader's name) _____. Keep him out of harm's way so that his health and safety are never threatened. I pray that there will be no attempt to take his life, and that absolutely no weapon formed against him will prosper. I pray for the protection of his wife and children, (names) _____. Shield them from any sickness, injury, or threats to their lives. Hide them all in the shadow of Your wing.

Lord, You have said that "if any of you lacks wisdom, let him ask of God, who gives to all liberally and without reproach, and it will be given to him" (James 1:5). On behalf of our leader, I pray for him to have wisdom, discernment, and knowledge for every decision he makes. Give him strength so he will not grow weary. Give him humility so he will not become proud. Give him direction so he will not lose his way. Give him favor with the people and other world leaders so he will be a uniter and not a divider.

Lord, Your Word says that the king's heart is in Your hand and like a river of water You turn it wherever You want (Proverbs 21:1). I pray that You would turn our leader's heart toward You at all times so that in the midst of the many voices he hears each day, he will still be able to hear Your voice far above them. Guide him in every situation.

Lord, I know that You establish the position of a leader who is true and fair to his people and who helps those who cannot help themselves (Proverbs 29:14). I pray that our leader will always do what is best for the people. Enable him to unfailingly be a leader who moves in the truth, because he has aligned himself with the Spirit of Truth. Cause him to build on the solid foundation of Your Word so that he will always be a solid leader.

I pray for each one of his advisors and counselors to have wisdom and always be able to give him the wise counsel he needs. Specifically I lift up to You (names of his advisors)

_____.

I pray that each one of these men and/or women will be people of integrity, honesty, discernment, and understanding. May their desire always be God's best for this nation. I pray that our leader and each of his counselors and advisors will come to a full knowledge of You and Your ways. May they seek Your wisdom in all matters "for wisdom is a defense as money is a defense, but the excellence of knowledge is that wisdom gives life to those who have it" (Ecclesiastes 7:12).

Lord, Your Word says, "There is a way that seems right to a man, but its end is the way of death" (Proverbs 16:25). I pray that our leader and his advisors will not just do what *seems* right, but will seek Your counsel so they will do that which they *know* is right in Your eyes. You have said that "without counsel, plans go awry, but in the multitude of counselors they are established" (Proverbs 15:22). I pray that our leader will have good counsel from *all* his advisors and that he will hear it. Show them what You want them to do, guide them in all decisions, give them answers and solutions. Most of all I pray that they would seek Your counsel, and that no decision would be made outside of Your will.

Give our leader clarity in his mind so that he is able to discern the truth from a lie. I know that when the leader is righteous, the people under him will be too. But "if a ruler pays attention to lies, all his servants become wicked" (Proverbs 29:12). May the president always recognize evil and call it what it is so that he will "reign in righteousness" and "rule with justice" (Isaiah 32:1). In Jesus' name I pray.

2. Pray for All Elected Officials

Lord, I pray that the people elected to office in our country will be godly and righteous men and women. Raise up men and women who are believers in You and cause them to find favor with the people so they will be voted into office. Give the voters discernment to distinguish the best person for the job.

I pray that every Christian will vote when the opportunity arises. Help us to see it as a chance to be Your hand extended in order to accomplish Your will on earth. Help us to be a powerful influence for good in our nation. Expose any corruption in the election process itself so that it can be made right.

Guide all voters to vote for the men or women who best represent Your purposes for this nation. Give the voters wisdom to know who the righteous leaders are and vote accordingly. Let there be clear signs of who is a good, godly candidate and who is not. Put a desire for godly leaders in the heart of each voter. Keep the people who are without integrity from being able to deceive the voters. Reveal the sins of those running for office so that people of evil intentions will not be elected. Spirit of Truth, I invite You to reign in this land and in the election process.

Lord, I pray for each of our leaders who represent us to have the wisdom they need to govern and make laws that are good. Specifically, I pray for (name elected officials)

_____.

May they seek You for wisdom, knowledge, and understanding. I pray that all men and women who represent the people will work together in unity to do what is best for our country. Let them be of one mind, without competition. The issues that are most pressing on my heart for my nation right now are (name specific issues)

_____

_____

_____.

I pray that these problems would be resolved in the best way possible. Show our representatives what that way is and lead them in it. Don't let them fail to do the things they should. Make them all to be men and women of integrity and honesty.

I pray that only righteous men and women will be in authority. For Your Word says, "When righteous people are in authority, the people rejoice" and "the righteous considers the cause of the poor, but the wicked does not understand such knowledge" (Proverbs 29:2,7). Fill our elected officials with the Spirit of truth. For I know that when the Spirit of truth has come, He will guide them into all truth (John 16:13).

I pray also for all leaders over every city and section of our country to be godly men and women of integrity, wisdom, and selflessness. Specifically I pray for (name the men and/or women who govern your city and section of the country).

_____

_____

_____.

Give each one wisdom and help them to lead in truth, honesty, and the fear of God. In Jesus' name I pray.

3. Pray for All Judges and People Involved in the Courts of Law

Lord, I pray that only *righteous* judges would be in this position in our nation. May each one be a godly person who loves Your laws. I pray they will meditate on *Your* laws before they interpret the laws of the land. Give every judge the wisdom and integrity to judge righteously so they will never violate Your laws, and may Your will be done in each decision they make.

Give wisdom to our leaders who make decisions regarding who our judges are. May they always choose people who are righteous. Don't allow anyone who is opposed to Your ways to get into that position.

Lord, I pray that You would expose all dishonest, corrupt, or evil judges in our country. Bring their sins to light so that their evil will not prosper. You have said that, "he who rules over men must be just, ruling in the fear of God" (2 Samuel 23:3). I pray for each judge in our nation to be filled with the fear of God. May they also be filled with fear over what the consequences would be for ungodly, dishonest, or corrupt behavior on their part. Help them to "judge righteously, and plead the cause of the poor and needy" (Proverbs 31:9). In Jesus' name I pray.

4. Pray for the Military

Lord, I pray that You would help us to develop and maintain a strong and skilled military. Guide all of our military leaders. Specifically, I lift up to You <u>(names of military leaders)</u>

_____

_____.

Give them godly wisdom to make the right decisions in defending our country. Give them revelation to know the plans of any enemy even before an attempt is made to carry them out.

Protect all of the people in our armed forces. Give them courage, faith, and clarity of mind to do their job perfectly. When they must go into battle, put a hedge of protection around them. Surround them on all sides and let no weapon formed against them prosper. Give them strength to endure. Be their hiding place and shield. Uphold them according to Your Word that they may live. Help them to know there is hope in You and if You hold them up, they will be safe (Psalm 119:114-117). May the funds our armed forces need for the tasks at hand and the equipment they must have be provided for them so they can excel.

Bring about in this nation an attitude of great respect and honor for all who are serving in the military and for those who have served in the past. For each one injured in the line of duty, I pray Your hand of healing and grace be upon them. Reward them in every way for the job they have done. I pray for the families of those who have died in combat or while on duty. Give them Your peace, provision, comfort, blessing, and a special sense of Your presence.

For anyone who is taken captive as a prisoner of war by the enemy, I pray that You would set them free unharmed. Give them strength to endure and comfort to know that You will rescue them. For anyone who is imprisoned for their faith, protect and deliver them from the hands of the enemy. For any who are missing in action, make a way for them to be found. Comfort their families as they wait for word.

When we must be at war, I pray it will be as bloodless as possible and that we will be victorious according to your will. Protect every man and woman engaged in the battle. Guide all military leaders with strategies that are impeccable, precise, and supremely effective. Help them to find and destroy the evil enemy before the enemy can destroy other people. I pray that our fighting men and women will not become casualties of war. To all the men and women of our military who are risking their lives for their country this day, I say to you, "be strong and of good courage, do not fear nor be afraid of them; for the LORD your God, He is the One who goes with you. He will not leave you nor forsake you" (Deuteronomy 31:6). "If God is for us, who can be against us?" (Romans 8:31).

Bring a Holy Spirit-inspired revival to all of our military people. Revive their marriages and pour out Your Spirit upon their families. Enable them to see Your truth so they can come into a full knowledge of who You are. Give them a sense of the high purpose You have for each one of them. In Jesus' name I pray.

5. Pray for an End to Crime and Terrorism

Lord, I pray that You would move Your hand against the evil in our land. Expose the plots of men who plan crimes and acts of terrorism. May all their schemes be thwarted and come to nothing. Reveal to the authorities every detail of any terrorist plot against our country and its citizens here and abroad, so they can be stopped from carrying out their evil acts. Enable the authorities to find and apprehend them *before* they have accomplished their acts of terror.

Help all political leaders and law enforcement and intelligence agencies of this country to have the wisdom and revelation they need to rid our land of criminals and terrorists and their threats against us. Enable them to see potential problems before they become a danger. I pray for our law enforcement agencies that You would reinforce their ability to find, apprehend, arrest, and bring to conviction all criminals and terrorists. Teach them how to investigate and spot suspicious activity. Help them to find and capture all lawbreakers associated with such activity and bring these people to justice. Give them supernatural abilities to uncover evil before it has had a chance to destroy people and property. I call upon You, Spirit of Truth, to guide these people in all truth (John 16:13).

Whenever retaliation is called for against evil men, let it be accurate, powerful, and devastating so that they will be severely discouraged from further pursuing such destruction. Open the blind eyes of the men who would carry out such evil and destruction. Awaken in them a conscience that would convict them of their evil and cowardly acts.

Even though our enemies hide so they cannot be seen, I know that You see everything. You know where these evil people are. Reveal their whereabouts to the men and women of our law enforcement agencies and enable them to apprehend them. Reveal details and important information and bring to light the deeds that are hidden. I say of all criminals and terrorists in this country that, "there is nothing covered that will not be revealed, nor hidden that will not be known.

Therefore whatever you have spoken in the dark will be heard in the light, and what you have spoken in the ear in inner rooms will be proclaimed on the housetops" (Luke 12:2-3).

Enable all law enforcement men and women to do their jobs with integrity and honesty. Expose those who are corrupt or who do not uphold the high standards of a civilized society so they can be removed. Bless those greatly who do their jobs well. In Jesus' name I pray.

6. Pray for the Spiritual Life of the Nation

Lord, I pray for an outpouring of Your Spirit upon our nation. Bring revival into every city and town in every part of our country and into every church. I pray that there will be no dead churches, but only churches that are filled with new life in You. I pray for unity in the body of Christ. Help us to proclaim the gospel as revealed in Your Word so that the eyes of the blind will be opened to see who You really are. Bring millions of people into Your kingdom through faith in Jesus Christ. Let this revival be so powerful that it affects every part of our nation and touches every part of the world.

Raise up Christian leaders and pastors in this country who will not compromise their integrity and who will resist the temptation to be immoral or disobedient to Your laws. Give them revelation so that they will have the perfect words at the right time. Give them a powerful voice to speak into the lives of millions of people, especially in times of tragedy or national concern when their ears and minds are open to hear. Help them to point people in the right direction so they can lift the standard of morality far higher than it has been. Enable them to lead people into a closer relationship with the living God so that this country will become a God-fearing nation.

We confess that as a nation we have been a rebellious people who have doubted You and made light of Your laws. Forgive us for shutting You out of our lives. We confess as the body of Christ that we have not always maintained consistent commitment in prayer. Our prayers have been powerless because we have not always lived and prayed Your way. Remove the blinders from our eyes where we are deceived. Help us to move out of our darkness and into Your light so we can be Your light extended to others. Teach us how to "not be overcome by evil, but overcome evil with good" (Romans 12:21).

Lord, I pray that You would remove the veil of doubt that has blinded the minds of the people who don't know You. Specifically I lift to You the unbelievers of our nation. Lord, I know that "if our gospel is veiled, it is veiled to those who are perishing, whose minds the god of this age has blinded, who do not believe, lest the light of the gospel of the glory of Christ, who is the image of God, should shine on them" (2 Corinthians 4:3-4). I know that if people could really see You for who You are, they would see the light and not reject You. Reveal Yourself to them. Open their eyes so that they "may see wondrous things from Your law" (Psalm 119:18). And for those who know the Scriptures but don't know You, reveal Jesus, the living Word, and make Your Word come alive to them.

I pray for millions of people to receive Jesus as Savior. Specifically I lift up to You (name specific unbelievers by name) _____

_____.

Reveal Yourself to them. Send believers into their lives to speak to them about You in a way that opens their eyes to Your goodness. Bring them into a full knowledge of Jesus as Savior. Lord, You have said that "whoever calls on the name of the Lord shall be saved" (Romans 10:13). I pray that men and women everywhere will call on Your name and be saved.

Lord, Your Word says "where there is no revelation, the people cast off restraint; but happy is he who keeps the law" (Proverbs 29:18). I pray for a revelation of Yourself to people so that they will love Your law and reject anything that is not Your way. Set us free from people who try to keep us from speaking about You. Deliver people who have a form of godliness but deny its power (2 Timothy 3:5).

On behalf of our nation, I repent of pornography, racism, prostitution, abortion, robbery, greed, idolatry, murder, sexual sins, lust, covetousness, adultery, and faithlessness (list any other sins you recognize in your nation) _____

_____

_____

_____.

Deliver us from the consequences of them. Convict the hearts of people who engage in these things. Bring them to their knees in repentance before You.

Lord, I know Your heart is moved with compassion for Your people who are "weary and scattered, like sheep having no shepherd" (Matthew 9:36). And You are not willing that any should perish but that all should come to repentance (2 Peter 3:9). Send out laborers into the harvest, Lord. Remind us as Your people to pray "always with all prayer and supplication in the Spirit, being watchful to this end with all perseverance and supplication for all the saints" (Ephesians 6:18). Help us to open our mouth and speak boldly about the wonders of You. In Jesus' name I pray.

7. Pray for a Strong Economy

Lord, Your Word says that You are the one "who gives power to get wealth" (Deuteronomy 8:18). And when You give wealth, You don't bring sorrow with it (Proverbs 10:22). And You say that being greedy for gain takes away from our lives (Proverbs 1:19). Help us to find that balance where we are not greedy for gain, but as we do our work enable us to receive financial rewards and blessings from it.

In that same way I pray for our nation's economy. Make it strong and stable. Keep it from getting out of control so that people's lives are not destroyed. Especially protect people living in poverty, or on the edge of it, who would be most painfully affected by a slipping economy. I pray that You would put godly and brilliant men in the positions of making decisions about our nation's economy. Give them vision to foresee the future and wisdom to make the right choices concerning it. Show them what the consequences will be for their actions.

I pray that we will not follow the gods of money and materialism. Let us not be a people who "trust in their wealth and boast in the multitude of their riches" (Psalm 49:6). I pray instead that we will be a people who look to You for our blessings. Establish us as a holy people to Yourself, as You have promised to do if we keep Your commandments and walk in Your ways. May we be people who lend and do not borrow, who give as You direct us. Bless Your people with the riches You want us to have, so that we in turn will be able to bless others. In Jesus' name I pray.

8. Pray for Educators, Teachers, and Students

Lord, I pray that Your name and Your laws will be lifted up in the classrooms of this nation, from the earliest grades through the graduate schools. We know that it was You, Lord, who brought down the Berlin Wall after so many of us in the body of Christ prayed for years for it to be destroyed so that our brothers and sisters behind the Iron Curtain would be free to worship You. In that same way bring down the wall of secularism in our schools. May that wall crumble to the ground and liberate the people imprisoned by it.

Lord, I pray that You would remove all evil influences from our schools. Let every plan of the enemy be exposed. I pray that no weapons will be allowed to prosper in any school in this nation. Expose every evil plan brewing in the mind of any student. Keep people with evil intentions away from school grounds. Bring back the fear of the Lord onto our campuses and with it a respect for human life.

Lord, give all teachers, educators, and anyone in authority in every educational facility the wisdom to lead and instruct. Raise up godly teachers and leaders. For those who are in charge of the education system on the local, state, and national levels, give them wisdom to make godly choices. Remove those who are opposed to Your ways and raise up believers to fill those positions. Bring a revival of godliness and Holy Spirit-led life into our schools, so that students may become educated in moral values as well as intellectual development. Make our schools a place where there is joy in learning. Strengthen the discipline practices so that students who are disruptive can be corrected or removed. Establish order and a respect for authority into the classroom.

Lord, I pray that You would also give our young people great respect for the laws of our country and all who are in authority, from policemen and political officials to the leader of our nation. Help them to learn respect for others by what they are taught by their parents and teachers. Raise up godly young people who are inspired to excel for the purpose of becoming all God made them to be. May they desire wisdom, knowledge, instruction, and understanding. May they seek justice and equity for all. Give our children, teenagers, and young people a vision of how they can serve You and make a difference. May they not be self-absorbed, but rather God-absorbed. I pray that they would find the things of the world to be empty and disappointing.

Our young people are the hope of our nation, and we will not give them up to the devil and his works of darkness. Lord, I pray that the minds and souls of our young people be secured in Your hands. Help us to bring up our children to have wisdom beyond their years so that we can become a nation wise beyond what we have ever known. I speak to our nation according to Your Word that "all of your children shall be taught by the LORD, and great shall be the peace of your children" (Isaiah 54:13). In Jesus' name I pray.

9. Pray for God's Protection on Our Land

Lord, I pray that You would protect our country from evil enemies. Surround our borders and protect us from invasion. Defend us from any enemy who would try to destroy our nation and its people or overtake our nation from within. Specifically I ask that You would protect us from terrorist attacks of any kind. Do not allow evil men to kill and destroy. Reveal their plans before they are put into action. Let all their attempts to destroy and paralyze this country with fear be completely stopped.

I pray that any attempt to deliver weapons of mass destruction to our land would be thwarted. Specifically, I pray that any attempt to use chemical, biological, or nuclear warfare against us would fail. I bind the enemy working through evil men and say that no weapon formed against us shall prosper. I stand against the enemy who would spread fear, panic, or anxiety among us. Our trust is in You, Lord. Protect us from all the plots of evil men.

Protect all of our ambassadors overseas. Surround our embassies with Your arm of protection. Make our embassies and ambassadors symbols of peace and light to the people of the countries they are in. Expose any plans of evil that seek to destroy these places of refuge or anyone in them.

When disasters do happen in our country, I pray that You would enable all service and law enforcement agencies to work together to do everything necessary to come to the aid of those who need it. Help them to arrive quickly and rescue the victims. Bless our relief organizations so they will have the workers and supplies they need. Help them to feed, clothe, and give refuge to those who need it. Protect all firefighters, policemen, and emergency workers as they do their jobs so that their lives are not sacrificed. Show us how to pray in these situations and how we can be of service in these crisis times. May Your Holy Spirit bring comfort to all who are suffering.

Lord, give our leader and his advisors the wisdom to navigate any rough waters our nation experiences. Help them to make quick decisions according to Your will and Your ways. Show them the wise things to do and the precautions to take in order to ensure our safety. Guide the people who make decisions regarding security so that they can install the most effective measures for protecting the people of our country.

I especially pray for security on the airlines. I pray that there will not be any hijacked planes, bombs on planes, crashed planes, or crimes committed on planes or at airports anywhere in our nation or in the world. May all plans of evil men be revealed before they can carry them out. "My defense is of God, who saves the upright in heart" (Psalm 7:10).

I pray according to Your Word that in righteousness we will be established. We shall be far from oppression, and we will not fear. We will be far from terror, for it will not come near us. Evil people who assemble against us will fall (Isaiah 54:14-15). I pray that we as a nation and as individuals will lie down in peace, and sleep; for You alone, O LORD, make us to dwell in safety (Psalm 4:8). God, You are our refuge and strength, a very present help in trouble (Psalm 46:1). "I will lift up my eyes to the hills—from whence comes my help? My help comes from the LORD, who made heaven and earth" (Psalm 121:1-2). Help us to "dwell in a peaceful habitation, in secure dwellings, and in quiet resting places" (Isaiah 32:18). In Jesus' name I pray.

10. Pray for National Unity

Lord, You have said that if even just two of us can agree about anything we ask that You will do it. I see how important it is for people to be in agreement and unity. I pray that You would instill in every citizen the desire to be in unity with everyone else. May there be mutual respect, friendship, and brotherly love among the people of this land. Help us each to do our part to bring peace on earth. Give us a national conscience to clearly distinguish right from wrong with regard to how we treat one another, and work in us a willingness to choose the right way. Give us "a good conscience, in all things desiring to live honorably" (Hebrews 13:18).

Just as in a healthy family we learn to appreciate each member's uniqueness because we want to preserve the family, I pray that in the family of our nation there would also arise appreciation and respect for the uniqueness of each individual. Help us to celebrate our differences as qualities that keep life interesting. Specifically I pray that all racial hatred and discrimination be completely uprooted, exposed, and eliminated. May the fire of Your Holy Spirit burn and destroy such ignorance and cruelty. Break down the barriers that divide every ethnic and racial group in this nation.

Lord, You have said in Your Word "how good and how pleasant it is for brethren to dwell together in unity" (Psalm 133:1). Help us to be unified with each other in our families, our marriages, and our communities. Help us to be unified with our leaders. Keep our leaders in a place of unity among themselves. I stand against the plans of the enemy to bring division within our country and pray that disunity will never be allowed to tear our country apart.

Where it has become fashionable to criticize leaders or people who are different from us, may it become an embarrassment to those who do it. Lord, I know Satan comes to destroy by dividing and to create disharmony through ignorance and hatred. I pray that Your Spirit of love and respect would prevail in this country instead. I pray that we will be called the "Repairer of the Breach" (Isaiah 58:12). In Jesus' name I pray.

11. Pray for the Media

Lord, I pray for all those who work in the media. They have been granted unique power and influence. I pray that You would be in charge of the airwaves and raise up godly people to fill all positions in that industry. Whether they work for newspapers, magazines, radio, television, or films, remove everyone who desires to promote evil and their own selfish agenda.

Work in the people of this nation a desire for truth. Weed out those in the media who would taint their news reports according to their own fleshly desires. Give wisdom to those who report the news so that they will not report things that are untrue, or that will endanger the lives of others. Where the media tries to stir up division, I pray that those media people will be rooted out. Instead, elevate those in the media who want to report the truth and be of service to humanity.

I pray for producers and directors of motion pictures and television programs to be convicted when they attempt to put out products that exalt sin and mock godliness. Give them a conscience to understand the consequences for misusing the power and influence they have been given. I pray an end to coarse and vulgar language, violent and repulsive acts, and explicit sexual scenes that grieve the Holy Spirit. I pray that the body of Christ will rise up to pray against this flooding of our culture with the ugliness from the realm of darkness.

I pray for an end to entertainment that glorifies evil and all that is base and godless. I know that "righteousness exalts a nation, but sin is a reproach to any people" (Proverbs 14:34). I pray that You would remove unrighteousness from our land. Sift out those who desire to bring us down, and either convict them of the errors of their ways or release them from their positions of influence. In their place elevate to positions of power the many talented people who want to create products that will elevate, encourage, comfort, heal, grow, instruct, and enlarge us. May the media become a powerful force for good instead of evil. In Jesus' name I pray.

12. Pray for the Nations of the World

Lord, I know that what happens in our country affects other nations. And what happens in other nations of the world affects us, too. That's why I pray for peace and harmony between our country and all other countries of the world. I am grateful that You have said in Your Word that with You, nothing is impossible. You are the God of the impossible. So I ask for what is impossible without Your miraculous power: peace on earth.

Lord, Your Word says that you remove kings and raise up kings (Daniel 2:21). I pray that you would remove any evil ruler, and deliver all people who are suffering under cruel dictators. Raise up righteous and godly leaders to be in control in each country. Your Word says, "it is an abomination for kings to commit wickedness, for a throne is established by righteousness" (Proverbs 16:12). Wherever there is a country with an unrighteous government and evil, cruel, and unrighteous leaders, I pray You would destroy their rulership and replace them with men of integrity and godly vision. Bring all countries together to cooperate in order to root out terrorist organizations. Raise up men and women to be leaders of each country who will not stand for brutality, persecution, murder, terrorism, and corruption to flourish. Specifically I name (name countries and rulers) _____

_____

_____

_____.

Where there are people groups who are being persecuted, deliver them from the hands of their oppressors. Specifically I pray for_____

_____.

Send Your servants into every nation of the earth to teach them about Jesus and Your ways. Open the eyes of any nation who doesn't know You. I pray an end to false religions that hold people in bondage. Break the hold these false religions have and open the eyes of the people to the truth of Your

Word. Pour out Your Spirit in every country and every city and on every government and leader. Reveal the truth of who You are to them. Specifically, I pray that You would send missionaries, evangelists, and Christian workers to (name countries)

_____

_____.

Raise up men and women in the body of Christ whom You would have go. Help these servants You send to "go into all the world and preach the gospel to every creature" (Mark 16:15). Put Your Spirit upon them and anoint them to preach the gospel to the poor. Send them to "heal the brokenhearted," to "proclaim liberty to the captives," and "recovery of sight to the blind." Help them to "set at liberty those who are oppressed" (Luke 4:18). Protect Your servants from persecution. Be with them as You send them to "make disciples of all the nations" (Matthew 28:19).

Lord, You are the light of the world, and I declare You to be Lord over every nation of the earth. I know Your light shines in darkness and the darkness does not comprehend it (John 1:4-5). But I know Your light will always prevail. Establish Your kingdom on earth. In Jesus' name I pray. Amen.

Weapons of Warfare

I exhort first of all that supplications, prayers, intercessions,
and giving of thanks be made for all men, for kings and all
who are in authority, that we may lead a quiet and peaceable
life in all godliness and reverence. For this is good and
acceptable in the sight of God our Savior, who desires all
men to be saved and to come to the knowledge of the truth.
1 Timothy 2:1-4

The work of righteousness will be peace, and the effect of
righteousness, quietness and assurance forever.
Isaiah 32:17

You shall seek them and not find them—
those who contended with you. Those who war
against you shall be as nothing, as a nonexistent thing.
For I, the Lord your God, will hold your right hand,
saying to you, "Fear not, I will help you."
Isaiah 41:12-13

Take away the wicked from before the king,
and his throne will be established in righteousness.
Proverbs 25:5

Be anxious for nothing, but in everything by prayer
and supplication, with thanksgiving, let your requests
be made known to God; and the peace of God,
which surpasses all understanding, will guard
your hearts and minds through Christ Jesus.
Philippians 4:6-7

Specific Prayer Needs and Answers to Prayer

Use these remaining pages to write down any specific prayer needs the Holy Spirit shows you. Don't forget to include answers to prayer as well.

OTHER BOOKS BY STORMIE OMARTIAN

THE POWER OF A PRAYING® WIFE

Stormie shares how wives can develop a deeper relationship with their husbands by praying for them. Packed with practical advice on praying for specific areas, including decision-making, fears, spiritual strength, and sexuality, this book will help women discover the fulfilling marriage God intended.

THE POWER OF A PRAYING® HUSBAND

Building on the success of *The Power of a Praying® Wife*, Stormie offers this guide to help husbands pray more effectively for their wives. Each chapter features comments from well-known Christian men, biblical wisdom, and prayer ideas.

THE POWER OF A PRAYING® PARENT

Stormie offers 30 easy-to-read chapters that focus on specific ways to pray for children. This personal, practical guide leads the way to enriched, strong prayer lives for parents.

JUST ENOUGH LIGHT FOR THE STEP I'M ON

Stormie has put together this collection of devotional readings perfect for the pressures of today's world. New Christians and those experiencing life changes or difficult times will appreciate her honesty, candor, and advice based on experience and the Word of God.